CONTEMPORARY TOPICS 1

INTERMEDIATE LISTENING AND NOTE-TAKING SKILLS

SECOND EDITION

HELEN SOLÓRZANO

LAURIE FRAZIER

MICHAEL ROST
SERIES EDITOR

Longman

longman.com

Contemporary Topics 1: Intermediate Listening and Note-Taking Skills
Second Edition

Pearson Education, 10 Bank Street, White Plains, NY 10606

Vice president, publishing: Allen Ascher
Senior acquisitions editor: Virginia Blanford
Development director: Penny Laporte
Development editors: Stacey Hunter, Lise Minovitz
Vice president, director of design and production: Rhea Banker
Executive managing editor: Linda Moser
Production manager: Ray Keating
Production editor: Michael Mone
Director of manufacturing: Patrice Fraccio
Senior manufacturing buyer: Dave Dickey
Photo research: Tara Maldonado
Cover design: Elizabeth Carlson
Cover image: Artville.com
Text design: Debbie Iverson
Text composition and art: Color Associates
Text Illustrations: **22** Dusan Petricic

Photo credits: **1** © Gregg Segal/Getty Images/Stone; **10** left: © B. Borrell
Casals/Frank Lane Picture Agency/CORBIS; center: © Doug Wilson/COR-
BIS; right: © Skip Nall/Getty Images Inc./PhotoDisc, Inc.; **18** Artist,
Cosimo Cavallaro, courtesy of Sarah Jacobs; **23** top left: UN/DPI Photo; top
right: UN/DPI Photo; bottom left: UN/DPI Photo; bottom right: Collection
Walker Art Center, Minneapolis, Gift of Frederick R. Weisman in honor of
his parents, William and Mary Weisman, 1988; **27** © S. Morris/CORBIS;
35 © Peter Cade/Getty Images, Inc.; **43** Will Faller 1995; **51** Nick
Koudis/Getty Images; **59** Richard Hutchings; **69** © David Hanover/Getty
Images/Stone; **78** © David & Peter Turnley/CORBIS; **87** left: © Catherine
Panchout/Getty Images, Inc.; center: © Chris Falkenstein/Getty Images,
Inc./PhotoDisc, Inc.; right: © Ken Fisher/Getty Images, Inc.; **94** John W.
Mauchly Papers, Rare Book & Manuscript Library, University of
Pennsylvania

Library of Congress Cataloging-in-Publication Data

ISBN 0-13-094853-5

Printed in the United States of America
1 2 3 4 5 6 7 8 9 10–BAH–05 04 03 02 01

CONTENTS

Scope and Sequence iv

Acknowledgments vi

Preface to the *Contemporary Topics* Series vii

Introduction ix

Unit 1 Happiness 1

Unit 2 New Kinds of Food 10

Unit 3 Public Art 18

Unit 4 Journey to Antarctica 27

Unit 5 Violence on Television 35

Unit 6 Too Old to Learn? 43

Unit 7 Are We Alone? 51

Unit 8 Do the Right Thing 59

Unit 9 A Good Night's Sleep 69

Unit 10 Negotiating for Success 78

Unit 11 Risking It 87

Unit 12 The Electronic Brain 94

Appendix A: Academic Word List 103

Appendix B: Affix Charts 109

Scope and Sequence

Unit	Topic	Note-Taking Tip
1 **Happiness**	Psychology	Note main ideas and details
2 **New Kinds of Food**	Biology	Note subtopics
3 **Public Art**	Art	Note descriptions
4 **Journey to Antarctica**	History	Note dates and events
5 **Violence on Television**	Media Studies	Note numbers
6 **Too Old to Learn?**	Linguistics	Listen for signal phrases
7 **Are We Alone?**	Astronomy	Listen for rhetorical questions
8 **Do the Right Thing**	Ethics	Note definitions
9 **A Good Night's Sleep**	Public Health	Note causes and effects
10 **Negotiating for Success**	Business	Note examples
11 **Risking It**	Statistics	Note comparisons and contrasts
12 **The Electronic Brain**	Technology	Choose the best note-taking techniques

Corpus-Based Vocabulary	Projects
achieve / assume / attitudes / factors / positive	Discussing proverbs about happiness Conducting interviews about happiness
benefit / consume / dominate / environment / normal	Giving a presentation about genetically modified food Researching a genetically modified food
concept / features / illustrate / interpret / promote	Planning a piece of public art Researching an artist
approached / area / despite / goal / proceed	Evaluating supplies Researching a famous explorer
assess / estimate / focused / impact / long-term	Debating violence on TV Observing violence on TV
conclude / evidence / period / remove / theory	Expressing opinions about skills Researching critical skills in animals
approximately / investigate / locate / range / restricted	Choosing items to send on a rocket Conducting a survey
analyze / individual / justify / principle / source	Discussing ethics and lying Researching an ethical decision
consequence / creates / function / require / survey	Creating a poster about sleep advice Keeping a sleep diary
affects / communicate / conflict / issue / react / techniques	Researching negotiating techniques in different cultures Role playing a negotiation
circumstances / injure / occur / perceived / significant	Ranking the risk of activities Conducting a risk perception survey
complex / designed / error / previous / technology	Discussing the effects of computers Researching an invention

Acknowledgments

The series editor, authors, and publisher would like to thank the following consultants, reviewers, and teachers who offered invaluable insights and suggestions for the second edition of the *Contemporary Topics* series: Michele Alvarez, *University of Miami;* Dorothy Avondstrondt, *University of Miami;* Cynthia Bermudez, *University of Miami;* Ana Maria Bradley Hess, *Miami-Dade Community College;* David Burger, *Seigakuin University;* David Chatham, *Osaka YMCA International College;* Mary Erickson, *Wichita State University;* Heidi Evans, *Wisconsin English as a Second Language Institute;* Carole Franklin, *University of Houston;* Charlotte Gilman, *Texas Intensive English Program;* Talin Grigorian, *American English Institute;* Aaron Grow, *Pierce College, Washington;* Adele Hanson, *University of Minnesota;* Patty Heiser, *University of Washington;* Funda Jasanu, *Yeditepe University, Istanbul, Turkey;* Greg Jewell, *Drexel University;* Lorne Kirkwold, *Hokkai Gakuen University;* Oswaldo Lopez, *Miami-Dade Community College;* Diane Mahin, *University of Miami;* Michele McMenamin, *Rutgers University;* Donna McVey, *Drexel University;* Masanori Nishi, *Osaka YMCA International College;* Patrick O'Brien, *Hokkai Gakuen University;* Gary Ockey, *International University of Japan;* Bivin Poole, *Osaka YMCA International College;* Kathy Sherak, *San Francisco State University;* Eiji Suenaga, *Hokkai Gakuen University;* Margaret Teske, *Mount San Antonio College;* Bill Thomas, *Wichita State University;* Margery Toll, *California State University at Fresno;* James Vance, *ELS Language Center, St. Joseph's University;* Susan Vik, *Boston University;* Andrea Voitus, *California State University at Fresno;* Cheryl Wecksler, *Drexel University;* and Jean Wiulson, *Toyo Eiwa University.*

In addition, the authors of *Contemporary Topics 1* would like to thank Michael Rost for his leadership in this project. We would also like to thank Eleanor Barnes, Stacey Hunter, and Lise Minovitz at Pearson Education for all their valuable suggestions during development. Finally, we would like to thank our families for supporting us during our work.

LONGMAN ON THE WEB

Longman.com offers classroom activities, teaching tips and online resources for teachers of all levels and students of all ages. Visit us for course-specific Companion Websites, our comprehensive online catalogue of all Longman titles, and access to all local Longman websites, offices, and contacts around the world.

Join a global community of teachers and students at Longman.com.

Longman English Success offers online courses to give learners flexible, self-paced study options. Developed for distance learning or to complement classroom instruction, courses cover General English, Business English, and Exam Preparation.

For more information visit EnglishSuccess.com.

Preface to the *Contemporary Topics* Series, Second Edition

As many language teachers now realize, listening is not simply an important skill. It is also a critical basis for progress in language learning. Effective listening enhances students' abilities to pay attention, remember new grammar and vocabulary, process ideas, and respond appropriately. As students develop their listening abilities, they feel more capable and confident in all aspects of language use.

Students at different levels need different kinds of listening skills and strategies, but most eventually encounter the need for academic listening. More than merely enabling them to succeed in college lectures and discussions, effective academic listening allows students to build, synthesize, and use knowledge in the target language. As a result, they can fully participate in the exchange of authentic ideas about relevant topics.

Recent progress in language teaching and testing has provided many new instructional approaches and strategies that help students develop good academic listening skills. *Contemporary Topics*, a three-level audio and text series, incorporates these new ideas into a coherent, carefully sequenced approach that works well in a variety of classrooms.

Authentic Language and Active Listening

Each level of the series comprises twelve original lectures on relevant contemporary topics drawn from a range of academic disciplines, accessible to students of all backgrounds. In a feature new to this edition, the lectures are recorded in an interactive style that models both the natural, authentic language of academic lectures and the active listening of students questioning and responding to the speaker. In addition, the lectures include explicit discourse markers that guide understanding. Key points are also reinforced so that they are easier to remember.

The activities that accompany each lecture are designed to slow down the listening process. Students are encouraged to preview vocabulary, listen with a clear purpose, take notes efficiently, organize and review their notes, and apply the content. The activities also help students develop critical thinking skills, including:
- activating prior knowledge
- guessing meaning from context
- predicting information
- organizing ideas
- discriminating between main ideas and details
- reconstructing and summarizing main ideas
- transferring knowledge from lectures to other areas

The Academic Word List

Because *Contemporary Topics* is designed as a bridge to the world of content listening, at least half the target vocabulary in each lecture is drawn from the latest academic word corpora. The Academic Word List in Appendix A, developed by Averil Coxhead, consists of ten sublists containing the most commonly used academic vocabulary. Of these lists, Sublist 1 contains the most frequently used words, Sublist 2 the next most frequently used, and so on. *Contemporary Topics 1* includes words from Sublists 1–4, *Contemporary Topics 2* includes words from Sublists 5–7, and *Contemporary Topics 3* includes words from Sublists 7–10. As students progress through the series, they internalize the vocabulary they need to understand academic lectures on a wide range of topics.

In addition to the Academic Word List, the Affix Charts in Appendix B provide a useful tool for building academic vocabulary.

Although the lectures and activities in this series provide the basis for learning, the key to making *Contemporary Topics* work in the classroom is involvement. Listening is an active process that involves predicting, guessing, interacting, risk-taking, clarifying, questioning, and responding. The authors and editors of *Contemporary Topics* have created a rich framework for making students more active, successful learners and teachers more active guides in that process.

Michael Rost, Ph.D.
Series Editor

Introduction

Contemporary Topics 1 is an intermediate level book and audio program created to develop academic listening and note-taking skills. The lectures are designed to give students an authentic listening experience while building the skills and linguistic knowledge they need in order to understand what they hear. Lecture topics, from a variety of academic disciplines, were selected because of their high interest to students. The lectures are presented in an authentic style and represent a variety of rhetorical structures that mirror the lectures a student will encounter in an academic environment.

To build academic listening skills, *Contemporary Topics 1* helps students:
- learn academic vocabulary that will be useful in many future contexts
- become familiar with a variety of rhetorical structures and the discourse cues those structures evoke
- explore how to organize notes for different types of lectures
- build comprehension by listening to short, clear lectures while taking notes
- use the information from their notes to reconstruct the lecture
- evaluate which listening strategies and note-taking styles work best for each individual

Organization of Units

The Student book contains twelve units. The units are sequences, but each can stand on its own. Each unit has six sections: Topic Preview, Vocabulary Preview, Taking Better Notes, Listening to the Lecture, Using Your Notes, and Projects.

Topic Preview   Each unit opens with one or more pictures that introduce the topic of the lecture. By spending a few minutes talking about the pictures, students begin to predict the content of the lecture. The Topic Preview questions can be discussed in pairs or small groups. This section introduces the topic, stimulates interest, and elicits background knowledge and vocabulary related to the topic.

Vocabulary Preview   This section contains three parts that help prepare students by previewing the academic vocabulary specific to the lecture. The first part presents ten key words in context, half of which are from the Academic Word List. In the second exercise, students use the words again in a new context in order to better understand the meaning. The final exercise gives students practice in recognizing the new vocabulary words as they are pronounced in natural speech.

Taking Better Notes   Note-taking is an important skill, but it can be overwhelming at the lower levels. This section aims to teach students practical strategies before they listen to the lecture. Students learn to recognize the discourse markers that signal the rhetorical features, such as exemplification or comparison and contrast, which appear in a lecture. They then look at a page of example notes, which show them how to organize this type of information on the page.

Listening to the Lecture This section contains three parts: Before You Listen, Listening for Main Ideas, and Listening for Details. In Before You Listen, students answer simple questions to help them make predictions about the topic of the lecture. In Listening for Main Ideas and Listening for Details, the procedure has changed from the first edition. In order to make the listening task more authentic, students are asked to close their books and take notes while they listen. They then open their books and answer the comprehension questions based on their notes. This explicit requirement—to use lecture notes to answer questions—further emphasizes the importance of good note taking.

Using Your Notes This new feature in *Contemporary Topics 1* encourages students to evaluate how well they have applied the note-taking strategies. Students work with their own notes and the notes of other classmates to fill in summaries of a lecture, put the ideas on note cards, and make diagrams and charts of the information—all authentic tasks that students use to study from notes. By finding out how well their notes help them with these tasks, students are encouraged to evaluate their own note taking process to find out what works best for them. In addition, they can check the cumulative Note-Taking Tips list, which summarizes the note-taking strategies presented throughout the book.

Projects The projects in this section allow students to use the information they learned in the lecture by applying and extending it in new ways. Typical activities include discussions, surveys, role-plays, and presentations. Each unit contains at least one project that can be done in class and one that requires some research outside the class.

To the Student

The goal of *Contemporary Topics 1* is to help you improve your academic listening and note-taking skills. Using this book will help you increase your vocabulary, improve your listening comprehension, take better notes, and use the information in your notes.

Increase Your Vocabulary

You will learn vocabulary from the Academic Word List. This is a list of the most common words used in academic texts. You will hear these words again and again in lectures and textbooks.

Improve Your Listening Comprehension

The best way to improve your listening comprehension is to practice listening. Listening will become easier with practice. The lectures in this book are similar to lectures you might hear in a lecture class, but are shorter and easier to understand.

Take Better Notes

You use several skills when you take notes. You have to listen to a lecture, understand it, and write down the important information in a very short amount of time. This book will teach how to recognize the organization of a lecture, and how to use the organization to help you take notes. However, remember that everyone takes notes differently. Try the new techniques presented in this book, but think about what works best for you.

Use the Information in Your Notes

You will learn to use your notes in many ways. First, you will use them to answer questions about the main ideas and details in the lecture. Then you will review your notes and use them to make outlines, charts, or summaries of the information in the lecture. You will also have a chance to talk about the information and use it in new ways.

Helen Solórzano
Laurie Frazier

Psychology

Happiness

Topic Preview

Work in small groups. Discuss the questions below.

1. Look at the picture. What happened to this person? Why is he happy?

2. How happy are you today—very happy, a little happy, or unhappy? Why?

3. What are three things that make you feel happy?

Vocabulary Preview

A The boldfaced words below are from a lecture about happiness. Read each sentence. Circle the letter of the word or phrase that is closest in meaning to the boldfaced word.

1. If you want to *achieve* in school, you have to work hard.

   To *achieve* means to _____ something.

   a. succeed at
   b. not do
   c. think about

2. I'm very tall, so people always *assume* that I play basketball. Actually, I hate basketball and never play it.

   To *assume* something means to _____.

   a. tell the truth about something
   b. ask a question about something
   c. think that something is true

3. Successful students have good *attitudes*. They enjoy school, and they want to learn.

   Your *attitude* is the way you _____ something

   a. think and feel about
   b. learn about
   c. try to do

4. When deciding to buy a house, you must think about many *factors*, including the location, price, and neighborhood.

   A *factor* is one of many things that _____ a situation.

   a. proves something about
   b. influences or causes
   c. stops or slows down

5. I don't play the piano well now, but I'll *improve* if I play every day. I hope to play well by the end of the year!

   To *improve* means to _____.

   a. become better
   b. become worse
   c. remain the same

6. He is having problems now, but he's **_optimistic_**. He thinks his problems will get better.

Being **_optimistic_** means you believe that _____ things will happen.

   a. good
   b. bad
   c. unusual

7. It is easy to see children's **_personalities_**. Some children are shy and some are very friendly.

Your **_personality_** is the way you _____ other people.

   a. talk about
   b. like
   c. act with

8. I think we will find a solution to this problem. I have a **_positive_** feeling about it.

A **_positive_** feeling is a _____ feeling.

   a. bad
   b. complicated
   c. good

9. She has a great **_relationship_** with her sister. They are good friends and love each other very much.

A **_relationship_** is the _____ between people.

   a. distance
   b. connection
   c. difference

10. I'm **_satisfied_** with my life now. I'm happy and I don't want anything to change.

To be **_satisfied_** means to be happy because something _____.

   a. will change very soon
   b. is how you want it
   c. makes other people happy

B Circle the letter of the word that best completes each sentence.

1. Having enough money and being healthy are two _____ that help make people happy.
   a. factors
   b. personalities

2. When I have a test, I never _____ it will be easy. That's why I always study a lot.
   a. positive
   b. assume

3. I worked hard on the project, and I am _____ with the job I did.
   a. satisfied
   b. achieved

4. My family and I have a very close _____.
   a. relationship
   b. attitude

5. I am very _____ about this class; I know I'll do well.
   a. improved
   b. optimistic

C Listen to each sentence and repeat it. Try to pronounce the boldfaced word correctly.

1. He wants to *achieve* a lot this year.

2. They *assume* I play basketball.

3. He has a good *attitude* about school.

4. Think about all the *factors* before you decide.

5. I'll *improve* if I play every day.

6. He's *optimistic* about the future.

7. Children's *personalities* form at a young age.

8. I have a *positive* feeling about it.

9. She has a close *relationship* with her sister.

10. I'm *satisfied* with my life.

Taking Better Notes

Noting Main Ideas and Details

Taking organized notes is a very important skill. It can help you focus on the main ideas of the lecture and remember the information later.

One way to organize your notes is to write the main ideas on the left side of the page. Then indent the details (facts and examples) below the main ideas.

Read the notes from a lecture about happiness. Notice how the student used the symbols below.

= equals; is   + and; plus

WHAT IS HAPPINESS?
Feeling happy = physical (body) + psychological (mind)
Physical =
    smiling
    slow heartbeat
Psychological =
    not worried
    thinking clearly

Work with a partner. Use the above notes to answer the questions below.

1. What is the lecture about?

2. Where are the main ideas?

3. Where are the details?

When you listen to a lecture, try to separate the main ideas from the details in your notes. Use symbols, if possible.

Listening to the Lecture

Before You Listen

You will hear a lecture about happiness. Check (✓) two topics you think the speaker might discuss.

_____ Family

_____ Money

_____ Success in school

_____ Personality

_____ Good health

Listening for Main Ideas

A Close your book. Listen to the lecture and take notes.

B Use your notes. Check (✓) the three most important factors for happiness. Compare your answers in small groups.

_____ Having a lot of money

_____ Being satisfied with yourself

_____ Being optimistic

_____ Being successful at work or school

_____ Being healthy

_____ Having good relationships

Listening for Details

🎧 **A** Close your book. Listen to the lecture again. Add details to your notes and correct any mistakes.

B Use your notes to decide if the statements below are true or false. Write T (true) or F (false).

_____ 1. Psychologists talked to hundreds of people to find out why they were or weren't happy.

_____ 2. Happy people don't want to change anything about their lives.

_____ 3. Unhappy people think they will be happy if something changes.

_____ 4. Happy people usually don't have problems.

_____ 5. Unhappy people are optimistic about their problems.

_____ 6. Having close relationships is not an important factor for achieving happiness.

_____ 7. Unhappy people have fewer close relationships than happy people.

_____ 8. Money is an important factor for achieving happiness.

Using Your Notes

A Look at Before You Listen on page 6. Did the speaker discuss the topics you checked?

B Work with a partner. Use your notes. Complete the outline on page 8 with the correct personality factors below. Add one detail about each personality factor.

always want to change	assume things will get worse
optimistic	few friends
~~satisfied with themselves~~	many close relationships

HAPPY PEOPLE

1. Satisfied with themselves

    Feeling comes from inside, not outside

2. _____
                      (1)

   _____
                      (2)

3. _____
                      (3)

   _____
                      (4)

UNHAPPY PEOPLE

1. _____
                      (5)

   _____
                      (6)

2. _____
                      (7)

   _____
                      (8)

3. _____
                      (9)

   _____
                    (10)

C Look at the Note-Taking Tip below. How can you improve your notes the next time you listen to a lecture?

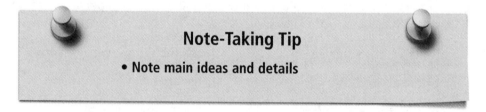

Note-Taking Tip

• Note main ideas and details

D Rewrite or revise your notes to make them clear. If you need to, listen to the lecture again.

Projects

1. Read the proverbs. Then answer the questions that follow.

    Where there is love, there is happiness. (Poland)

    Happiness does not often come with an empty stomach. (Japan)

    Happiness and glass break easily. (Denmark)

    You can never be happy if you make others unhappy. (China)

    It is better to have a piece of bread with a happy heart than to have a lot of money with sadness. (Egypt)

    True happiness comes from giving it to others. (India)

    a. What does each proverb mean? Do you agree with it? Why or why not?
    b. Do you know any other proverbs about happiness? If so, explain them.
    c. Do you think any of the proverbs support the ideas in the lecture? If so, which ones?

2. Interview three people outside of class about what makes them happy. Circle Male or Female. Ask them to rank each factor from 1 (very important) to 3 (not very important). Write their answers in the chart.

Factors	Male / Female	Male / Female	Male / Female
Loving family			
Lots of money			
Good friends			
Interesting work			
Good health			
Positive attitude			

    Then discuss your interview results in a small group. What factors were most important? Why? Did men and women answer differently? Explain.

3. What is your opinion of the personality factors described in the lecture? Do you agree that they are the most important factors for happiness? Explain.

New Kinds of Food

Topic Preview

Sometimes scientists change plants in the laboratory. These changes make them grow differently from normal plants. We call food from these plants *genetically modified (GM) food.*

Work in small groups. Discuss the questions below.

1. Look at the pictures. Do you think any of these foods have been changed? If so, how?

2. How can you tell if food has been modified?

3. Would you eat genetically modified food? Why or why not?

Vocabulary Preview

A **The boldfaced words below are from a lecture about genetically modified food. Read each sentence. Cross out the word or phrase that is *different* in meaning from the boldfaced word.**

1. I *altered* the plans for my garden. Instead of planting flowers, I decided to plant vegetables.
   a. changed
   b. kept
   c. modified

2. Weeds have started to *dominate* my garden. I need to pull them out so the flowers and vegetables won't die.
   a. control
   b. take over
   c. remove

3. I don't like to use chemicals that harm the *environment* on my plants. These chemicals can get into the water we drink and the food we eat.
   a. land, sea, and air
   b. earth and soil
   c. houses and buildings

4. I grow a lot of my own fruits and vegetables because I like to eat *fresh* food.
   a. new
   b. old
   c. just picked

5. It is good to eat fruits and vegetables. One *benefit* is that you get a lot of vitamins.
   a. helpful thing
   b. advantage
   c. problem

6. Corn is planted in the spring and *harvested* in the late summer.
   a. picked
   b. left
   c. collected

7. My strawberry plants don't look *normal*. They are too small and they haven't grown any fruit.
   a. different
   b. as expected
   c. usual

8. I try to kill the insects in my garden without using *pesticides*.
   a. chemicals
   b. poison
   c. seeds

9. Farmers who work with chemicals have a *risk* of getting sick.
   a. safety
   b. danger
   c. chance

10. Some countries *consume* more food than they can produce.
    a. eat
    b. grow
    c. use

B Read each group of sentences. Circle the letter of the sentence that is closer in meaning to the first sentence.

1. I altered my plans.
   a. I changed my plans.
   b. I kept my plans the same.

2. Mary tries to dominate the other students in our class.
   a. Mary tries to work with her classmates.
   b. Mary tries to control her classmates.

3. I don't like to work in a noisy environment.
   a. It's difficult for me to work in a noisy place.
   b. I don't like to make a lot of noise.

4. I like fresh fruit, not fruit from a can.
   a. I don't like food that is cold.
   b. I like food that has just been picked.

5. There are many benefits to exercising every day.
   a. Exercising every day is fun.
   b. Exercising every day is good for you.

6. I harvested the apples.
   a. I planted them.
   b. I picked them.

7. She put pesticides on her vegetable garden.
   a. She used chemicals to protect her vegetable garden from insects.
   b. She used chemicals to make her plants grow faster.

8. I don't like to take a lot of risks.
   a. I like danger and excitement.
   b. I like to be safe.

9. People living near the ocean consume a lot of fish.
   a. People who live by the ocean go fishing a lot.
   b. People who live by the ocean eat a lot of fish.

10. I had a normal day today.
    a. I had a usual day.
    b. I had an unusual day.

C Listen to each sentence. Circle the word you hear.

1. altered   normal

2. pesticides   dominate

3. consume   environment

4. fresh   risk

5. harvest   benefits

6. pesticides   environment

7. altered   normal

8. harvest   fresh

9. benefits   risks

10. dominate   consume

Taking Better Notes

Noting Subtopics

In many lectures, the speaker discusses more than one subtopic of a topic. For example, the speaker may talk about something's benefits and risks. This type of lecture is usually divided into two or more parts. Each part discusses a different subtopic.

First, the speaker introduces the subtopics:

> Today, I'm going to talk about the pros and cons of growing genetically modified foods.
> Now, we'll discuss some of the benefits and risks of genetically modified food.

There may be more than one idea about each subtopic. The phrases below introduce new ideas about each subtopic.

> One (idea) . . .
> Another (idea) . . .
> A third (idea) . . .
> A final (idea) . . .
> The most important (idea) . . .

Read the notes from a lecture. Notice how the two subtopics (benefits and risks) are labeled and separated.

GROWING ORGANIC FOOD   (organic = with no pesticides)

Benefits
    1. no toxic chemicals on food
    2. doesn't harm environment

Risks
    1. plants may not grow well
    2. insects may eat plants

Work with a partner. Use the above notes to answer the questions below.

1. What is this lecture about?

2. The notes are divided in two parts. What are the two parts?

3. How many benefits are there to growing organic food? How many risks?

When you listen to a lecture, try to clearly label and separate different subtopics. Use symbols, if possible.

Listening to the Lecture

Before You Listen

You will hear a lecture about the benefits and risks of GM food. Write one benefit and one risk you think the speaker might discuss.

Benefit: _____

Risk: _____

Listening for Main Ideas

A Close your book. Listen to the lecture and take notes.

B Use your notes. Check (✓) three benefits and three risks of GM food discussed in the lecture. Compare your answers in small groups.

Benefits

_____ **a.** need fewer pesticides

_____ **b.** grow better

_____ **c.** need fewer farmers

_____ **d.** stay fresh longer

_____ **e.** healthier to eat

Risks

_____ **a.** more expensive

_____ **b.** dominate other plants

_____ **c.** hurt wild animals and insects

_____ **d.** hurt farm animals

_____ **e.** harmful to people

Listening for Details

A Close your book. Listen to the lecture again. Add details to your notes and correct any mistakes.

B Use your notes to complete each sentence below. Circle the correct answer.

1. Genetically modified <u>corn / tomato / strawberry</u> plants kill insects that eat the plants.

2. Genetically modified <u>corn / tomato / strawberry</u> plants grow in cold weather.

3. Genetically modified <u>corn / tomato / strawberry</u> plants stay fresh for two months.

4. Genetically modified <u>corn / tomato / strawberry</u> plants may dominate other plants.

5. Genetically modified <u>corn / tomato / strawberry</u> plants may kill butterflies.

6. Genetically modified <u>corn / tomato / strawberry</u> plants have genes from a fish.

Using Your Notes

A Look at Before You Listen on page 14. Did the speaker discuss the benefit and risk you wrote?

B Work with a partner. Use your notes to complete the outline below. Write the benefits, risks, and examples.

BENEFITS

1. Need fewer pesticides

   Example: _____

   (1)

2. _____

   (2)

   Example: Strawberries grow in cold weather

3. Stay fresh longer

   Example: _____

   (3)

RISKS

1. _____

   (4)

   Example: Tomatoes stronger than other plants

2. Hurt wild animals and insects

   Example: _____

   (5)

3. _____

   (6)

   Example: Strawberries have genes from fish

C Work in small groups. Use your notes to retell the lecture.

D Look at the Note-Taking Tips below. Did you use any of them when you took notes? Which were most helpful? How can you improve your notes the next time you listen to a lecture?

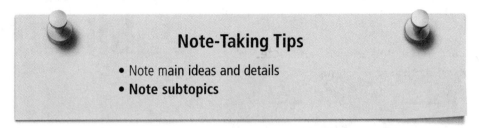

Note-Taking Tips

- Note main ideas and details
- **Note subtopics**

Projects

1. Make two lists. In one list, write the possible benefits of genetically modified food. In the other list, write the possible risks. Give a two-minute presentation. Explain whether you think growing genetically modified food is a good idea.

2. Use the Internet or library to research one type of genetically modified food. Give a short report to the class.

3. Scientists use many different kinds of genes to modify food. Does the kind of gene used affect your opinion about genetically modified food? For example, would you eat a tomato with a gene from another tomato? A potato? A fish? Bacteria? Explain.

Public Art

Topic Preview

Work in small groups. Discuss the questions below.

1. Look at the picture. Describe the sculpture. What do you think it is made of? How big do you think it is? What does it look like? What do you think it means?

2. Do you like the sculpture? Why or why not?

3. Check (✓) the kinds of art you like. Explain why you like them.

_____ art that looks real	_____ unusual art
_____ colorful art	_____ art that means something
_____ modern art	_____ paintings
_____ old or traditional art	_____ sculptures

Vocabulary Preview

A The boldfaced words below are from the lecture. Read each sentence. Circle the word or phrase that is closest in meaning to the boldfaced word.

1. The Statue of Liberty is **huge**. You can see it from very far away.
   a. very large
   b. beautiful
   c. well-known

2. I have a painting of my mother that is very **realistic**. It looks just like her.
   a. lifelike
   b. ugly
   c. unusual

3. René Magritte made **surrealistic** art. One famous painting shows men falling from the sky.
   a. truthful
   b. historical
   c. strange

4. In Leonardo Da Vinci's painting, Mona Lisa's **features** look very real, especially her eyes.
   a. parts of the face
   b. articles of clothing
   c. colors and shades

5. She told me a story to **illustrate** her point. After that, I understood her clearly.
   a. confuse
   b. show
   c. write

6. Teachers need to have a clear **concept** of the subject they are teaching.
   a. question
   b. education
   c. idea

7. The two countries' leaders tried to make **peace**. They wanted to stop the fighting.
   a. an international problem
   b. an end to war
   c. a part of a country

8. Our city leaders **promote** the arts. For example, they give a lot of money to musicians and artists.
   a. help
   b. dislike
   c. enjoy

9. I can't **interpret** this poem. I don't know what the poet means.
   a. understand
   b. organize
   c. read

10. To many Americans, the eagle **symbolizes** freedom.
    a. means
    b. fights
    c. gives

B Circle the letter of the word that best completes each sentence.

1. The painting is so _____ that it covers the whole wall.
   a. realistic
   b. huge

2. I don't really like _____ art. I think it looks very strange.
   a. surrealistic
   b. feature

3. My professor uses a lot of examples to _____ her ideas.
   a. promote
   b. illustrate

4. I think the woman in the picture looks sad, but my friend thinks she looks angry. We _____ the look on her face differently.
   a. symbolize
   b. interpret

5. I think this sculpture is very beautiful, but I don't understand the _____ behind it.
   a. concept
   b. peace

C Listen to each sentence. Circle the word you hear.

1. concept   promote
2. realistic   symbolize
3. peace   features
4. illustrate   interpret
5. concept   surrealistic
6. features   peace
7. realistic   huge
8. illustrate   promote
9. interpret   features
10. surrealistic   symbolizes

Taking Better Notes

Noting Descriptions

In a lecture, a speaker may describe different types of the same thing. You need to note descriptive words and phrases to help you remember how something looks or sounds. The phrases below are used to introduce descriptions.

This is *(a size, color, shape, or age)*.
It looks like *(a person or thing)*.
It's made of *(materials)*.
It symbolizes *(an idea or concept)*.

One way to note descriptions is to write the thing described on the left. Then note descriptive words and phrases on the right. Drawing a picture can also help you remember what something looks like.

Read the notes from a lecture about the sculpture on page 18. Notice how the student noted the sculpture's name and description and also drew a picture. Also, notice how the student used the symbols and abbreviations below.

10' = 10 feet   lbs. = pounds
x = by   symb. = symbolizes

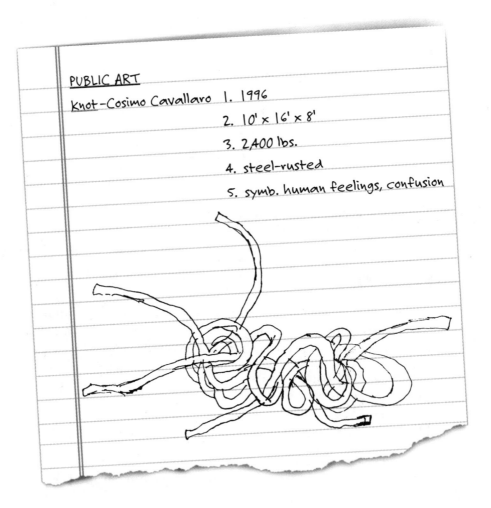

PUBLIC ART
Knot-Cosimo Cavallaro   1. 1996
                        2. 10' x 16' x 8'
                        3. 2,400 lbs.
                        4. steel-rusted
                        5. symb. human feelings, confusion

Work with a partner. Use the above notes to answer the questions below.

1. What's the name of this sculpture?

2. Who made it?

3. Describe the sculpture. Include its age, size, materials, and color.

4. What does this sculpture mean?

When you listen to a lecture, try to note descriptive words and phrases and draw pictures. Use symbols and abbreviations, if possible.

Listening to the Lecture

Before You Listen

You will hear a lecture about public art. Check (✓) the topics you think the speaker might discuss.

_____ The purpose of public art   _____ Famous modern artists

_____ The cost of public art   _____ Common styles of art

Listening for Main Ideas

A Look at the pictures. Listen to the lecture and take notes.

Peace

Let Us Beat Swords into Ploughshares

Non-Violence

Spoonbridge and Cherry

B The speaker described three of the sculptures on page 23. One was not mentioned. Use your notes. Number the pictures from 1 to 3 in the order they were described.

_____ Peace

_____ Let Us Beat Swords into Ploughshares

_____ Non-Violence

_____ Spoonbridge and Cherry

Listening for Details

A Close your book. Listen to the lecture again. Add details to your notes and correct any mistakes.

B Use your notes to decide if the statements below are true or false. Write T (true) or F (false).

_____ 1. Public art is found in museums.

_____ 2. Public art is becoming more popular.

_____ 3. Pop art is usually realistic.

_____ 4. One purpose of public art is to illustrate concepts.

_____ 5. The woman on the horse is a symbol for peace.

_____ 6. The sculpture _Non-Violence_ is an example of realistic art.

Using Your Notes

A Look at Before You Listen on page 23. Did the speaker discuss the topics you checked?

B Paraphrasing is explaining something in your own words. Work with a partner. Use your notes to paraphrase the lecture. Take turns completing the sentences below. Use the words in parentheses.

1. Public art is _____

   _____

   (*outdoors / public places / more popular*)

2. One purpose of public art is _____

   _____

   (*cities / beautiful / interesting / people / enjoy*)

3. One example is _____

   _____

   (Spoonbridge and Cherry / *huge / metal / sculpture / silver and red / pop art / everyday things*)

4. Another purpose of public art is _____

   _____

   (*illustrate / concepts / promote / beliefs*)

5. One example is _____

   _____

   (Peace / *woman / horse / realistic / symbol / peace*)

6. Another example is _____

   _____

   (Non-Violence / *metal / gun / knot / impossible / surrealism / promote / peace*)

C Look at the Note-Taking Tips below. Did you use any of them when you took notes? Which were most helpful? How can you improve your notes the next time you listen to a lecture?

Note-Taking Tips

- Note main ideas and details
- Note subtopics
- **Note descriptions**

D Rewrite or revise your notes to make them clear. If you need to, listen to the lecture again.

Projects

1. Work with a partner. Imagine that you are artists making a sculpture for a public place in your city. Draw a picture of your sculpture. Answer the questions below. Then present and explain your picture to the class.
   a. What is the sculpture called?
   b. What style is it? Pop? Realistic? Surrealistic?
   c. How big is it?
   d. What does it mean?
   e. Where do you want to display it?

2. Find a piece of public art you like. Look in your city or town (or conduct library or Internet research). Answer the questions below.
   a. What is the artist's name?
   b. Where is the artist from?
   c. When did the artist live?
   b. What style of art is it?
   e. Why do you like this art?

   Report your findings to the class. If possible, show a picture of the art.

History

Journey to Antarctica

Topic Preview

In 1914, explorer Ernest Shackleton began a journey to Antarctica. His ship was called the *Endurance*. We can see now that the name of his ship was a good description of his journey. *Endurance* means the ability to stay strong for a long time, even when you are in pain or have problems.

Work in small groups. Discuss the questions below.

1. What do you know about exploration in Antarctica?

2. Look at the picture of the ship *Endurance* in Antarctica. How do you think Shackleton and his crew kept warm? What do you think they ate?

3. Imagine that the ship was in trouble. What could the explorers do to help themselves? What other difficulties do you think the explorers had in Antarctica?

Vocabulary Preview

A The boldfaced words below are from a lecture about Shackleton's journey to Antarctica. Read each sentence. Guess the meaning of the boldfaced words.

1. As we *approached* the city, I started to see the lights from the houses and buildings.

2. There aren't any beaches in this *area*. You need to go somewhere else to go swimming.

3. *Despite* the bad weather, we enjoyed our trip. I had a really good time anyway.

4. My *goal* is to travel to Europe. I've always wanted to see it.

5. I'm going to *proceed* with my plans even if I have problems. I'm not going to quit.

6. My car got *stuck* in the mud, so I couldn't go anywhere.

7. The firefighter *rescued* the man from the burning house.

8. After a long day of hiking, we decided to set up *camp* for the night.

9. The boy put his toy boat on the lake and watched as it *floated* on the water.

10. We ran out of *supplies* on our camping trip. We didn't have any more food or water, so we had to go home early.

B Match each word with the correct definition.

_____ **1.** approach

_____ **2.** area

_____ **3.** despite

_____ **4.** goal

_____ **5.** proceed

_____ **6.** stuck

_____ **7.** rescue

_____ **8.** camp

_____ **9.** float

_____ **10.** supplies

a. things that you need for daily life

b. a place with tents where people stay for a short time

c. a particular part of a place

d. although something is true

e. staying firmly in one place and difficult to move

f. to stay on the surface of a liquid

g. to move closer to someone or something

h. to continue to do something that has already been started

i. to save someone from danger

j. something you want to do in the future

C Listen to each sentence and repeat it. Try to pronounce the boldfaced word correctly.

1. As we *approached* the city, I started to see lights from the buildings.

2. There aren't any beaches in this *area*.

3. *Despite* the bad weather, we enjoyed our trip.

4. My *goal* is to travel to Europe.

5. I'm going to *proceed* with my plans.

6. My car got *stuck* in the mud.

7. The firefighter *rescued* the man from the fire.

8. We set up *camp* for the night.

9. The boy watched his toy boat *float* on the lake.

10. We ran out of *supplies* on our camping trip.

Taking Better Notes

Noting Dates and Events

In a history lecture, the speaker often quickly says the dates of events (important things that happened). Writing dates will help you to remember the correct time and order of events.

The paragraph below gives dates and times of important events in Shackleton's life. Read the paragraph and the notes that follow. Notice how the student used abbreviations to note dates and events.

Ernest Shackleton was born in Ireland *on February 15, 1874. In 1890*, he went to sea. He was in the British Merchant Navy *for ten years* before his first expedition. He died *on the 5th of January, 1922*. Shackleton was one of the greatest explorers *of the twentieth century*.

SHACKLETON	
2/15/1874	Shackleton born
1890	Went to sea
10 yrs.	British Merchant Navy
1/5/1922	died
20th cent.	great explorer

Read the lecture excerpt. Underline the dates.

. . . Between 1907 and 1909, Ernest Shackleton led an expedition to the South Pole on a ship called the *Nimrod*. His goal was to be the first person to reach the South Pole. On August 7, 1907, he and his crew left London. In January 1908, the ship froze in the ice near the South Pole. The next day, Shackleton and his crew set up camp. On the 29th of October, 1908, they started for the South Pole, a 1700-mile round trip. They traveled over land for more than two months. By the 9th of January 1909, they were only 97 miles from the South Pole. But, sadly, they ran out of food and had to turn around, so they never achieved their goal. . . .

Read the student notes. Notice how the student used the symbols and abbreviations below.

r.t. = round trip   Exp. = Expedition
> = more than   S.P. = South Pole

```
                            Shackleton's Nimrod Exp.
        _____(1)_____
  Goal: 1st person to S.P.


        _____(2)_____   Left London

        _____(3)_____   Ship froze in ice

        _____(4)_____   Started for S.P. - 1700 miles r.t.

        _____(5)_____   Traveled over land

        _____(6)_____   97 miles from S.P. - turned around -

                            not enough food
```

The above notes are missing information. Use the dates below to complete them.

1/9/1909	1907-1909	1/1908
> 2 mos.	10/29/1908	8/7/1907

When you listen to a lecture, try to note important dates and events. Use symbols and abbreviations, if possible.

Listening to the Lecture

Before You Listen

You will hear a lecture about Ernest Shackleton's journey to Antarctica. Check (✓) the topics you think the speaker might discuss.

_____ Who went on the trip   _____ Why they went to Antarctica

_____ What supplies they took   _____ Who goes to Antarctica today

_____ How long the trip took

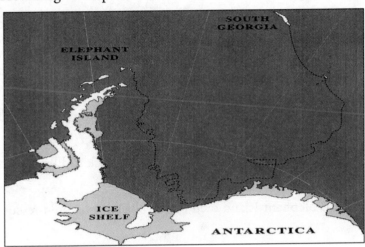

The Journey of the Endurance

Listening for Main Ideas

A Close your book. Listen to the lecture and take notes.

B Use your notes. Put the events below in the correct order. Number them from 1 to 7.

_____ The *Endurance* left South Georgia.

_____ Shackleton and his crew left for Elephant Island in three small boats.

_____ Shackleton's crew moved off the *Endurance* and camped on the ice.

_____ The *Endurance* became stuck in the ice.

_____ Shackleton and his crew reached the whaling station in South Georgia.

_____ Shackleton rescued all the men from Elephant Island.

_____ Shackleton and five men left Elephant Island to go to South Georgia.

Listening for Details

A Close your book. Listen to the lecture again. Add details to your notes and correct any mistakes.

B Use your notes to decide if the statements below are true or false. Write T (true) or F (false).

_____ 1. Shackleton's goal was to walk across Antarctica.

_____ 2. The *Endurance* left with a crew of 69 men and 20 dogs.

_____ 3. There was no ice in the water when the *Endurance* left South Georgia.

_____ 4. Shackleton and his crew lived on the *Endurance* for two weeks after it became stuck in the ice.

_____ 5. The crew camped on the ice for six months before they went to Elephant Island.

_____ 6. Shackleton and five men traveled over 800 miles from Elephant Island to South Georgia.

_____ 7. Shackleton waited three weeks before he went back to Elephant Island to rescue his crew.

_____ 8. The men on Elephant Island died before Shackleton could rescue them.

Using Your Notes

A Look at Before You Listen on page 31. Did the speaker discuss the topics you checked?

B Use your notes and the dates below to complete the notes on Shackleton's journey. Use abbreviations, if possible.

January 18	May 20	~~December 5~~
April 9	August 30	
April 24	October 27	

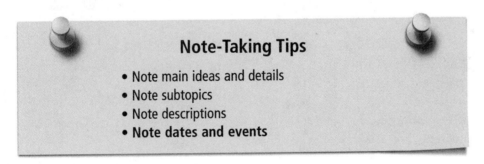

HISTORY: Endurance's journey → Antarctica

1914	Dec. 5 (1)	Endurance left S. Georgia.
1915	_____ (2)	Endurance got stuck in ice.
	_____ (3)	Crew left ship & camped on ice.
1916	_____ (4)	Crew took small boats to Elephant Island.
	_____ (5)	Shackleton & 5 men arrived at S. Georgia whaling station.
	_____ (6)	Shackleton rescued crew from Elephant Island.

C Look at the Note-Taking Tip below. Did you use any of them when you took notes? Which were most helpful? How can you improve your notes the next time you listen to a lecture?

Note-Taking Tips

- Note main ideas and details
- Note subtopics
- Note descriptions
- **Note dates and events**

D Rewrite or revise your notes to make them clear. If you need to, listen to the lecture again.

Projects

1. Work in a group. Imagine that you are part of Shackleton's crew. You need to decide which supplies to save from your ship before it sinks. You already have the food and water you need. You can take five more supplies. Choose the five supplies below that you think are most important.

tents	maps
sleeping bags	guns
sled dogs	fishing poles
cat	money
extra clothing	photos of family and friends
books and other reading materials	football

    Share your choices with the class. Explain why you chose them.

2. Read a library or Internet article about another famous explorer. Write a report about the explorer. Include the following information.

    a. What is the explorer's name?

    b. When did he or she live?

    c. Where did the explorer travel?

    d. What was his or her goal?

    e. Was he or she successful? Why or why not?

Media Studies

Violence on Television

Topic Preview

Work in small groups. Discuss the questions below.

1. Look at the picture. What kind of TV show do you think this child is watching? Why?

2. What are your opinions about TV? Complete each statement with an adjective below (or your own adjective).

fun	important	difficult	harmful
entertaining	educational	boring	silly
interesting	exciting	frightening	violent

a. I think that watching TV is _____.

b. Reading a book is more _____ than watching TV.

c. It is _____ for children to watch a lot of TV.

d. Seeing violence on TV may be _____ for children.

e. Many TV shows for children are _____.

Vocabulary Preview

A The boldfaced words below are from a lecture about violence on television. Read each sentence. Circle the letter of the word or phrase closest in meaning to the boldfaced word.

1. Killing is a more serious **act** of violence than hitting.
   An **act** is _____.
   a. something you do
   b. something you say
   c. something you think

2. The students took a test to **assess** their knowledge.
   To **assess** means to _____ something
   a. measure
   b. try
   c. agree on

3. The **average** adult in the United States watches three to four hours of television each night. However, some adults never watch television.
   An **average** person is _____.
   a. very young
   b. like most people
   c. very different

4. Mickey Mouse and Donald Duck are both cartoon **characters**.
   A **character** is _____.
   a. someone who watches TV
   b. someone in a story on TV
   c. someone who likes TV stories

5. We counted the hours of television a child watches each year. Then we counted the number of television commercials shown each hour. From this information, we **estimate** that a child sees about 30,000 commercials each year.
   To **estimate** means to _____ about something
   a. ask
   b. worry
   c. guess

6. The class discussion **focused** on how television affects children. For example, we talked about what children learn from TV.
   To **focus** means to _____ something.
   a. forget about
   b. pay attention to
   c. change to

7. When I asked a question, I got an *immediate* answer. I didn't have to wait long for the answer.
   Something *immediate* happens _____.
   a. after a long time
   b. tomorrow
   c. right now

8. Television commercials have a big *impact*. People buy things they see advertised on TV.
   An *impact* is _____.
   a. an effect
   b. a cause
   c. a mistake

9. There is a *link* between watching TV and bad health. When people watch a lot of TV, they eat more and get less exercise.
   A *link* is a _____.
   a. reason
   b. fact
   c. connection

10. When you make a decision, it's important to look at the *long-term* effects. Think about what will happen in a year or ten years.
    Long-term means _____.
    a. far in the future
    b. in a short time
    c. very important

B Circle the letter of the word that best completes each sentence.

1. We have a lot of topics to discuss, but first I want to _____ on the topic of TV violence.
   a. focus
   b. link

2. Let's think about the _____ effects that are far in the future.
   a. long-term
   b. immediate

3. In many cartoons, the _____ are animals.
   a. acts
   b. characters

4. I _____ that I watch about two hours of TV a day, but I'm not sure.
   a. average
   b. estimate

5. Watching TV commercials has an _____ on the things we decide to buy.
   a. impact
   b. assess

🎧 **C** You will hear each word below in a sentence. Listen to the sentences. Write the number of the sentence that contains each word.

_____ link

_____ focused

_____ assess

_____ long-term

_____ act

_____ impact

_____ average

_____ estimate

_____ characters

_____ immediate

Taking Better Notes

Noting Numbers

An important part of taking notes in many lectures is understanding and writing down numbers correctly. Numbers ending in –*teen* (for example, 13 or 14) sound very similar to numbers ending in –*ty* (for example, 30 or 40). To hear the difference, listen for syllable stress.

13 = thirTEEN   (stress on the last syllable)
30 = THIRty   (stress on the first syllable)

Work with a partner.

Student A: Read one list below. Don't tell your partner which list you read.

Student B: Close your book and write down the numbers you hear. Open your book and check your answers.

Then change roles.

List 1	List 2	List 3	List 4
13	13	30	30
40	14	40	14
50	15	15	50
16	60	60	16
70	70	17	17
18	80	18	80
19	19	90	90

Large numbers also include numbers ending in *-teen* and *-ty*. Notice how the syllables are stressed.

1,400 fourTEEN hundred	1,500 fifTEEN hundred
14,000 fourTEEN thousand	15,000 fifTEEN thousand
40,000 FORty thousand	50,000 FIFty thousand

Make a list of five large numbers. Include numbers with *-teen* and *-ty*.

Then work with a partner.

Student A: Read your list of numbers.

Student B: Take notes. Compare Student A's list with your notes.

Then change roles.

Listening to the Lecture

Before You Listen

You will hear a lecture about television and children. Which statements do you think are true? Write T (true) or F (false).

_____ 1. Most American families have a television.

_____ 2. American children spend more time at school than they do watching TV.

_____ 3. There is not much violence on children's TV shows.

_____ 4. When children watch a lot of TV violence, they become more violent as adults.

Listening for Main Ideas

A Close your book. Listen to the lecture and take notes.

B Use your notes. Put the topics in the order discussed in the lecture. Number the topics from 1 to 4. Compare your answers in small groups.

_____ Long-term effects of TV violence on children

_____ The amount of violence on TV

_____ Immediate effects of TV violence on children

_____ The amount of TV that American children watch

Listening for Details

A Close your book. Listen to the lecture again. Add details to your notes and correct any mistakes.

B Use your notes to complete the statements below. Circle a, b, or c.

1. In the United States, _____ percent of families have a TV.
   a. 52
   b. 90
   c. 98

2. American children watch _____.
   a. 3-4 hours of TV every day.
   b. 3-4 hours of TV every week.
   c. 30-40 hours of TV every week.

3. Children spend about _____ hours per year watching TV.
   a. 150
   b. 1,500
   c. 5,000

4. Children spend about _____ hours per year in school.
   a. 900
   b. 1,900
   c. 9,000

5. Cartoons have an average of _____ violent acts each hour.
   a. 3-4
   b. 30
   c. 32

6. By age 12, a child will see an average of _____ acts of violence on television.
   a. 1,000
   b. 100,000
   c. 10,000,000

7. Children saw someone hit and kick a doll on video. Then _____ percent of the children hit and kicked a real doll.
   a. 1
   b. 10
   c. 100

8. According to one study, when children watch a lot of TV at age 8, they are more violent at age _____.
   a. 14
   b. 18
   c. 28

Using Your Notes

Look at Before you Listen on page 39. According to the lecture, which statements are true?

B Read the summary of the lecture. Some information is wrong. Use your notes to correct the summary. Rewrite the summary with the correct information.

SUMMARY: TV VIOLENCE AND CHILDREN
— Almost 50% of American families have a television.
— Kids spend more time watching TV than
   going to school.
Research:
Amount of violence
— Cartoons have fewer acts of violence than adult
   TV shows.
— A child sees about 32 acts of violence on
   TV by age 12.
Immediate effects of TV violence
— Children copy the violence they see on TV.
      Ex. hit and kick a doll.
Long-term effects of TV violence
— When children watch a lot of TV, they have trouble
   in school when they are older.

C Look at the Note-Taking Tips below. Did you use any of them when you took notes? Which were most helpful? How can you improve your notes the next time you listen to a lecture?

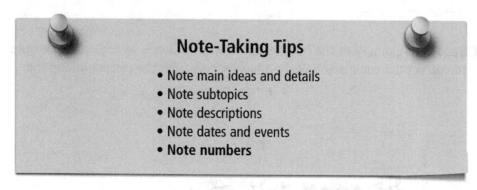

Note-Taking Tips

- Note main ideas and details
- Note subtopics
- Note descriptions
- Note dates and events
- **Note numbers**

D Rewrite or revise your notes to make them clear. If you need to, listen to the lecture again.

Projects

1. Divide the class into two teams. One team will argue that TV violence is responsible for violence in children. The other team will argue that it is not responsible. Use the ideas from the lecture and your own reasons to support your team's opinion.

2. Watch a children's cartoon or other television show for 15-30 minutes. Count how many acts of violence you see. Note the types of violence. Then discuss the questions below in class.

   a. What television show did you watch?

   b. Was the show for children, adults, or both?

   c. How many acts of violence did you see?

   d. Do you think children should watch this show? Explain.

   e. Do you think there is too much violence on TV? Explain.

   f. Do you think children should be protected from violence on TV? If so, who should protect them?

Linguistics

Too Old to Learn?

Topic Preview

Work in small groups. Discuss the questions below.

1. What do you think the children in the picture are studying? Why?

2. How old are they?

3. What is different about how adults and children learn?

Vocabulary Preview

A The boldfaced words below are from a lecture about how animals and humans learn. Read each sentence. Guess the meaning of the boldfaced words.

linguist

1. He can speak French, but he pronounces words with an American *accent*.
   way of speaking

2. *Adolescents* experience many changes as they grow up. They sometimes make the teenage years very difficult. *13 - 17*

3. Practice is *critical* for learning a new language. If you don't practice the language, you can't learn it. *imp.*

4. The research gives *evidence* about why some people learn languages more easily than others. *info that proves sth*

5. Monkeys and humans learn in different ways. We can therefore *conclude* that the human brain is different from a monkey's brain. *to decide sth is true from info*

6. To solve a problem, scientists first think of a *theory*. Then they do research to test if the theory is correct. *Idea / explanation may be true*

7. I'm going back to my *native* country to see my family. I miss my homeland. *where born*

8. John studied Chinese for a *period* of time. *length*

9. The students must *remove* their books from the desks before they take a test. *to take sth from where it is*

10. Learning a new language is like learning any new *skill*, such as driving a car or using a computer. It takes practice. *ability to do sth well*

B Match each word with the correct definition.

_____ 1. accent
_____ 2. adolescent
_____ 3. critical
_____ 4. evidence
_____ 5. conclude
_____ 6. theory
_____ 7. native
_____ 8. period
_____ 9. remove
_____ 10. skill

a. to decide that something is true from the information you have
b. a length of time
c. someone between 13 and 17 years old
d. an ability to do something very well, especially because you have learned it
e. relating to the place where you were born
f. a way of speaking that shows someone comes from a particular place
g. very important
h. words or facts that prove something
i. to take something away from where it is
j. an idea that tries to explain something, but it may not be true

C You will hear each word below in a sentence. Listen to the sentences. Write the number of the sentence that contains each word.

_____ conclude

_____ native

_____ skill

_____ accent

_____ critical

_____ remove

_____ period

_____ adolescents

_____ theory

_____ evidence

Taking Better Notes

Listening for Signal Phrases

How is a lecture organized? At the beginning of the lecture, speakers often outline the topics they will discuss. They may then say the order in which the topics will be presented. The signal phrases below are often used to organize the topics of a lecture.

First, I'd like to start by . . .
Then I'll talk about . . .
Finally, we'll look at . . .

During the lecture, speakers may use the signal phrases below to move from one topic to the next.

Now, let's move on to . . .
Now let's look at . . .

+ First
Second
Next
Finally

Read the introduction to a lecture about language learning below. Underline the signal phrases.

Today I'm going to talk about some new evidence about how we learn language. My discussion will be in three parts. First, I'll talk about how we learn our first language, or our native language, from our parents. Then, I'll discuss how we learn a second language. Finally, we'll look at the differences between learning a first and second language. . . .

Read the student notes on the lecture introduction. Notice how the student used the abbreviations below.

L = language   L2 = second language
L1 = first language   diff. = difference

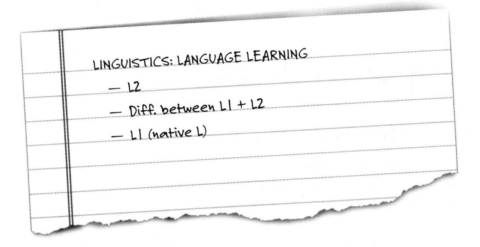

Some topics in the above notes are in the wrong order. Rewrite the notes in the correct order.

When you listen to a lecture, listen for signal words and phrases to help you expect what will be discussed. Use symbols and abbreviations, if possible.

Listening to the Lecture

Before You Listen

You will hear a lecture about how animals and humans learn. Check (✓) the statement you think might express the speaker's main idea.

_____ 1. Children and young animals learn more easily than adults.

_____ 2. Humans and animals do not learn in the same way.

_____ 3. Both humans and animals can learn languages.

Listening for Main Ideas

A Close your book. Listen to the lecture and take notes.

B Use your notes to complete the statements below. Circle a, b, or c. Compare your answers in small groups.

1. The critical period is the _____.
   a. age when someone becomes an adult
   b. time needed to learn a new skill
   c. reason why someone learns something new

2. According to the critical period theory, _____.
   a. children never speak with foreign accents
   b. people's brains change when they're adolescents
   c. adults can't learn a new language well

3. According to the lecture, humans must learn a second language before the critical period in order to speak it _____.
   a. fluently and easily
   b. without grammar mistakes
   c. with a native accent

Listening for Details

A Close your book. Listen to the lecture again. Add details to your notes and correct any mistakes.

B Use your notes to complete the statements below. Circle a, b, or c.

1. Songbirds have a critical period for learning to _____.
   a. sing
   b. fly
   c. build nests

2. Cats have a critical period for learning to _____.
   a. walk quietly
   b. use their eyes
   c. catch mice

3. _____ the critical period, animals cannot learn certain skills.
   a. After
   b. Before
   c. During

4. The critical period may explain why _____.
   a. adults can't learn new languages
   b. some languages are easier to learn
   c. children learn new languages easily

5. According to the speaker, adults may get frustrated while learning a new language because _____.
   a. they can't use it for daily life
   b. they can't pronounce the sounds correctly
   c. children can learn faster than they can

Using Your Notes

A Look at Before You Listen on page 47. Did the speaker express the main idea you checked?

B The lecture outline is missing information. Use your notes and the phrases below to complete the outline.

to sing	animals or humans	have light	to speak without accent
to see	hear parent's song	be young	

LINGUISTICS: CRITICAL PERIOD

1. Definition: Critical Period (C.P.)

   A time when _____ must learn something
                    (1)

2. Animals

   A. Songbirds

      C.P. for learning _____
                          (2)

      Must _____
                    (3)

   B. Cats

      C.P. for learning _____
                          (4)

      Must _____
                    (5)

3. Humans

   C.P. for learning _____
                          (6)

   Must _____
                  (7)

C Look at the Note-Taking Tips below. Did you use any of them when you took notes? Which were most helpful? How can you improve your notes the next time you listen to a lecture?

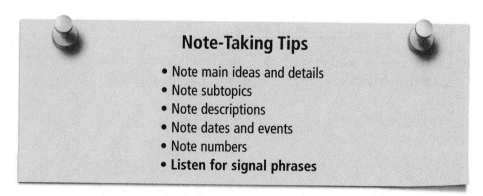

Note-Taking Tips

- Note main ideas and details
- Note subtopics
- Note descriptions
- Note dates and events
- Note numbers
- **Listen for signal phrases**

D Rewrite or revise your notes to make them clear. If you need to, listen to the lecture again.

Projects

1. Read the list of skills in the chart below. Put a check (✔) in the column that matches your opinion.

Skills	Must learn as a child	Is easier to learn as a child	Can learn as an adult
Walking			
Singing			
Playing the piano			
Swimming			
Riding a bicycle			

Compare and discuss your answers in a small group. Give examples to support your answers.

2. Choose an animal, bird, or insect that interests you. Conduct library on Internet research about a skill that is critical for this animal (for example, hunting or communication). Answer the following questions. Report your findings to the class.

    a. What animal did you learn about?

    b. What skill is critical for this animal? Why? Do both males and females learn this skill?

    c. How does the animal perform the skill?

    d. Do the parents need to teach their children this skill? If so, how do they teach them? Is there a critical period for learning this skill?

Astronomy

Are We Alone?

Topic Preview

Work in small groups. Discuss the questions below.

1. Look at the picture. What do you see? Do you think it is real?
    Why or why not?

2. Do you think there is intelligent life on other planets? Why or why not?

3. How can we look for other intelligent life in the universe?

Vocabulary Preview

A The boldfaced words below are from a lecture about astronomy. Read each paragraph. Match each boldfaced word with the correct definition.

Paragraph 1

How many (1) *galaxies* are in the universe? We think there are about 100 billion. All galaxies cover a very large area, but some are bigger than others. The smallest galaxies are (2) *approximately* one thousand (3) *light years* wide, and the largest are up to one million light years across. Every year, as astronomers look farther into the universe, they (4) *locate* new galaxies. After they find a new galaxy, they study it to learn more about the universe.

_____ **a.** to find where something is

_____ **b.** a little more or less than an exact number or amount

_____ **c.** large groups of stars and planets

_____ **d.** the distance that light travels in one year

Paragraph 2

How can we see galaxies? We can see other galaxies using a (1) *telescope*. Very large telescopes have a (2) *range* of hundreds of millions of miles, so we can see planets in other galaxies. There are also radio telescopes to listen for (3) *signals* or other sounds that are very far away.

_____ **a.** the distance that something can reach or travel

_____ **b.** sounds that tell you something

_____ **c.** an object that lets you see things that are far away

Paragraph 3

What do astronomers do? Astronomers (1) *investigate* the universe. They try to find out many different things. For some astronomers, research is (2) *restricted* to studying stars and planets; they don't study anything else. However, other astronomers also look for intelligent extraterrestrial life. They think there may be other intelligent (3) *beings* somewhere.

_____ **a.** people or living things

_____ **b.** to search for information about something

_____ **c.** controlled or limited

B Complete each sentence with the correct word from the box.

approximately	beings	galaxy	investigate	light years

1. I think people are the only intelligent _____ in the universe.

2. The Earth is only one of the planets in the Milky Way _____.

3. The nearest star (other than our Sun) is 4.2 _____ away from the Earth.

4. Astronomers plan to _____ new parts of the universe. They want to find out if there is any life there.

5. It would take _____ four years to get there, if you traveled at the speed of light.

locate	range	restricted	signal	telescope

6. My radio doesn't have a long _____. It can't get signals from far away.

7. Some scientists listen for a _____ from space. They want to know if other beings are trying to contact earth.

8. I looked for the star, but I couldn't _____ it in the sky.

9. The astronomy laboratory is _____. Only a few people can use it.

10. I like to look at the stars and planets through my _____.

C Listen to each sentence and repeat it. Try to pronounce the boldfaced word correctly.

1. There may be other intelligent ***beings*** in the universe.

2. There are many other ***galaxies*** in the universe.

3. The nearest star is 4.2 ***light years*** away.

4. Astronomers plan to ***investigate*** the universe.

5. It would take ***approximately*** four years to get there.

6. I can't get a ***signal*** on my radio.

7. My radio has a short ***range***.

8. I couldn't ***locate*** the star.

9. Our research is ***restricted*** to astronomy.

10. I like to look through my ***telescope***.

Taking Better Notes

Listening for Rhetorical Questions

One way that speakers introduce new topics is to ask rhetorical questions. The speaker does not expect an answer to this kind of question. Instead, the question is used to introduce an important idea in the lecture.

When asking a rhetorical question to introduce an idea, the speaker
- continues talking after the question
- does not look directly at students
- answers his or her own question

When a speaker expects you to answer a question, he or she
- stops talking after the question
- looks directly at the students
- asks follow-up questions, such as "Does anybody know?" or "What do you think?"

Read the beginning of a lecture about the SETI project. Underline the rhetorical questions.

Today we're going to talk about the SETI project. What does SETI stand for? The letters S-E-T-I stand for Search for ExtraTerrestrial Intelligence. Extraterrestrial means a being living on another planet. How did the SETI project begin? Well, the first ideas came in a paper published in 1958 by Giuseppe Cocconi and Philip Morrison, two physicists[1] from Cornell University. In this paper, the scientists suggested how we could search for intelligent life in the universe. Around that time, an astronomer named Frank Drake had the same idea, and in 1960 he began the first search. . . .

[1] scientists who study physical objects and natural forces such as light, heat, and movement

Work with a partner. Complete the lecture notes below. Use the correct rhetorical questions from the lecture on page 54.

ASTRONOMY: SETI PROJECT

_____
(1)
= Search for ExtraTerrestrial Intelligence
_____
(2)
-1958, Cocconi & Morrison-Cornell
-Drake—1960 first search

When you listen to a lecture, try to listen for rhetorical questions. Use the questions to identify and note important information. Use symbols and abbreviations, if possible.

Listening to the Lecture

Before You Listen

You will hear a lecture about the SETI project. Write two rhetorical questions you think the speaker might ask.

1. _____

2. _____

Listening for Main Ideas

A Close your book. Listen to the lecture and take notes.

B Use your notes. Number the rhetorical questions in the order asked in the lecture. Compare your answers in small groups.

_____ How does the SETI project look for other intelligent life?

_____ Why do scientists think there may be other intelligent beings in the universe?

_____ What is the range of radio signals in space?

_____ Why does the SETI project listen for radio signals from space?

Listening for Details

A **A** Close your book. Listen to the lecture again. Add details to your notes and correct any mistakes.

B Use your notes to complete the statements below. Circle a, b, or c.

1. There may be other intelligent life in the universe because there are _____.
   a. at least 100 billion galaxies in the universe
   b. signals coming to Earth from other intelligent beings
   c. a few planets that astronomers know will support life

2. The SETI project searches for extraterrestrial life by _____.
   a. listening for radio signals
   b. sending out radio signals
   c. sending rockets into space

3. According to the speaker, finding other intelligent life will _____.
   a. be very dangerous for our planet
   b. completely change the way we think
   c. help us learn more about space travel

4. Other intelligent beings may send messages on radio signals because the signals _____.
   a. are clear and easy to understand
   b. travel quickly and have a long range
   c. are easy to make and send

5. Traveling at the speed of light, it takes about _____ for a radio signal to reach Earth from the nearest galaxy.
   a. 4 years
   b. 4 thousand years
   c. 60 thousand years

6. Astronomers don't use rockets to look for intelligent life because they _____.
   a. travel much too fast
   b. are too expensive to build
   c. travel in only one direction

Using Your Notes

A Look at Before You Listen on page 55. Did the speaker ask the questions you wrote?

B Work with a partner. Use your notes to paraphrase the main ideas of the lecture. Take turns finishing the statements. Use the words in parentheses.

1. Many scientists think there may be other intelligent life in the universe

   because _____

   _____

   (*planet / star / galaxy / support life / similar*)

2. The SETI project searches for life by _____

   _____

   (*listening / radio / signal / telescope*)

3. The SETI research is exciting because _____

   _____

   (*locate / beings*)

4. The SETI project listens to radio signals because _____

   _____

   (*long / range / travel / quickly*)

5. Radio signals _____

   _____

   (*speed of light / light years / nearest galaxy*)

6. On the other hand, rockets _____

   _____

   (*10 miles per second / 60 thousand years / galaxy*)

7. Radio signals also _____

   _____

   (*range / distance / not restricted / area*)

8. Rockets _____

   _____

   (*restricted / direction*)

C Look at the Note-Taking Tips below. Did you use any of them when you took notes? Which were most helpful? How can you improve your notes the next time you listen to a lecture?

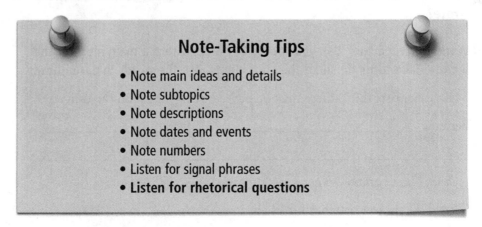

Note-Taking Tips

- Note main ideas and details
- Note subtopics
- Note descriptions
- Note dates and events
- Note numbers
- Listen for signal phrases
- **Listen for rhetorical questions**

D Rewrite or revise your notes to make them clear. If you need to, listen to the lecture again.

Projects

1. Imagine that your class is sending a rocket into space. Choose three objects to put in a small box inside the rocket. You hope other intelligent beings in the universe will find the box. You can include any type of object (for example, a photograph or computer disk), but everything must fit in the small box. Make a poster showing the objects you will send. Share your poster with the class and explain why you chose each object.

2. What do people think about the possibility of intelligent life in the universe? Ask the questions below to three people outside of class. Then share your results in a small group.
   a. Do you think there are other intelligent beings in the universe? Why or why not?
   b. What do you think these beings look like?
   c. Do you think any beings from other planets have visited earth? Why or why not?
   d. What will happen if we meet other beings? Will they be friendly or unfriendly? Explain.

Do the Right Thing

Topic Preview

Ethics tells us what is right and wrong. Ethics are the rules we live by.

Work in small groups. Discuss the questions below.

1. Look at the picture. What is happening? What do you think the girl should do?

2. How do you decide what is right and wrong? Religious teachings? Personal feelings? The law? Family beliefs? Something else?

3. Read the story. Is lying in this situation right or wrong? Explain.

    A woman is dying. She has 10,000 dollars in the bank, but she has no family. The woman tells a friend to spend all her money on a very expensive funeral. She tells him to buy a lot of flowers and an expensive coffin. The friend thinks this is a waste of money. He decides to use some of the money for a simple funeral, and then give most of it to a school for homeless children. However, he tells the woman that he will spend all the money on the funeral.

Vocabulary Preview

A The boldfaced words below are from a lecture about the ethics of lying. Read each sentence. Circle the letter of the word or phrase that best completes the sentence.

1. People have the *ability* to think and make decisions about their lives. Animals can't do this.
   An *ability* is the power to _____ something.
   a. do
   b. think about
   c. understand

2. For many people, religion is their *source* of ethics. Their religion tells them what is right and wrong, and they make decisions that follow those ideas.
   A *source* is _____.
   a. an important topic
   b. where something comes from
   c. the ability to understand

3. Before we talk about a solution, we need to *analyze* the problem. Then we'll know what we can do about all the parts of the problem.
   To *analyze* a problem means _____ it.
   a. open and look inside
   b. think carefully about
   c. find the answer to

4. There is a *common* belief that killing is wrong. Most people feel that this is true.
   A *common* belief is _____.
   a. not popular or usual
   b. difficult to understand
   c. shared by many people

5. After a person dies, the family comes together for a *funeral.* Then the person's body is buried or burned.
   A *funeral* is the _____ for a dead person.
   a. clothing
   b. songs
   c. ceremony

6. Each student in the class needs *individual* help. The teacher should work with each student alone, without the rest of the class.
Individual help is for _____.
   a. one person
   b. two people
   c. many people

7. Once you make a decision, you must *justify* it to others. For example, if you decide to stop going to school, you must explain why.
To *justify* means to explain _____.
   a. what you are doing next
   b. the reasons for something
   c. what something means

8. The teacher wanted her students to be kind to each other. She taught them to always follow this *principle*.
A *principle* is an idea that _____.
   a. makes you behave one way
   b. is the most popular
   c. makes a lot of money

9. It is important to *respect* other people's beliefs. For example, if your friend is a vegetarian, you should not serve him meat for dinner.
To *respect* someone's beliefs means _____.
   a. to ignore your own beliefs
   b. to try to change that person's opinion
   c. to not go against that person's wishes

10. I believe in the *right* of free speech. I think everyone should be able to say what he or she wants.
A *right* is something that _____.
   a. everyone wants to do
   b. no one should do
   c. everyone is allowed to do

B Complete each sentence with the correct word.

1. *right*   *ability*

   a. Unlike people, animals don't have the _____ to talk.

   b. I believe that every child has the _____ to go to school. Everyone should get an education.

2. *funeral*   *principle*

   a. After my father died, we had a small _____.

   b. I believe in the _____ that we should be kind to other people.

3. *analyze*   *justify*

   a. If I fail a test, I _____ my mistakes so I can understand what I did wrong.

   b. I didn't want to go to college right away, so I had to _____ my decision to my parents.

4. *respect*   *source*

   a. My parents are the _____ of my ethics. They taught me to be kind and truthful.

   b. I try to _____ people who are different from me. I want to understand their beliefs.

5. *common*   *individual*

   a. Each _____ person in the class has a different opinion. The students don't agree about many things.

   b. One _____ problem is making spelling mistakes. We all make these mistakes sometimes.

C You will hear each word below in a sentence. Listen to the sentences. Write the number of the sentence that contains each word.

_____ ability		_____ individual	
_____ source		_____ justify	
_____ analyze		_____ principles	
_____ common		_____ respect	
_____ funeral		_____ right	

Taking Better Notes

Noting Definitions

When giving lectures, speakers sometimes define key words or phrases. A speaker may introduce a key word or phrase by asking the questions below.

> What is X?
> How can we define X?
> What does X mean?

A speaker may also introduce a definition with the phrases below.

> X means . . .
> X is . . .
> Let's define X.

When noting definitions, write the key words or phrases on the left side of the page and the definition to its right.

Read the notes from a lecture about ethics. Notice how the student used the symbol below.

> → = then; causes

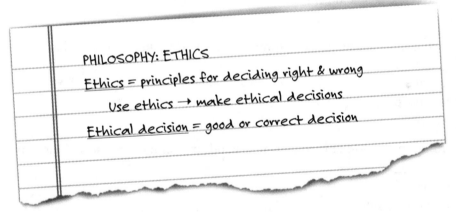

Work with a partner. Use the above notes to answer the questions below.

1. What words or phrases are defined in the notes? How do the notes show that these are important ideas?

2. Where are the definitions? How do the notes show that these are definitions?

When you listen to a lecture, try to note definitions. Use symbols and abbreviations, if possible.

Listening to the Lecture

Before You Listen

You will hear a lecture about the ethics of lying. Check (✓) the statement you think the speaker will make.

_____ Lying can never be justified.

_____ Lying can sometimes be justified.

_____ Lying can usually be justified.

Listening for Main Ideas

A Close your book. Listen to the lecture and take notes.

B Use your notes to complete the statements below. Circle a, b, or c. Compare your answers in small groups.

1. According to the principle of individual rights, you have the right to _____.
   a. do what is best for yourself
   b. make other people do things
   c. make your own decisions

2. According to the principle of common good, you should choose actions that help _____.
   a. everyone
   b. the most people
   c. yourself

3. According to the principle of common good, you should choose actions that harm _____.
   a. no one
   b. the fewest people
   c. anyone but you

Listening for Details

A Close your book. Listen to the lecture again. Add details to your notes and correct any mistakes.

B Use your notes. Decide if the statements below relate to individual rights or the common good. Check (✓) the correct box.

	Individual Rights	Common Good
1. This idea is based on the work of Immanuel Kant.	❏	❏
2. This idea is based on the work of Jeremy Bentham.	❏	❏
3. Lying is never ethical.	❏	❏
4. Lying is sometimes ethical.	❏	❏
5. Helping the school for homeless children is more important than telling the truth to the dying woman.	❏	❏
6. Telling the truth to the dying woman is more important than helping the school for homeless children.	❏	❏

Using Your Notes

A Look at Before You Listen on page 64. Did the speaker make the statement you checked?

B Many students find it helpful to write important information from their notes on note cards. Work with a partner. The note cards below are missing information. Use your notes to complete them.

Note Card 1

ETHICS: Rules we follow to decide right and wrong

PRINCIPLES OF INDIVIDUAL RIGHTS:

— Each person has the _____
(1)

to _____
(2)

_____

— Based on the work of Immanuel Kant

— Lying is always _____
(3)

Note Card 2

PRINCIPLE OF COMMON GOOD:

— Helps _____
(1)

— Harms _____
(2)

— Based on the work of Jeremy Bentham

Lying is sometimes wrong

Note Card 3

```
    EX.
    DYING WOMAN'S MONEY
       Individual Rights
       — Friend should _____
                                    (1)
           because _____
                                    (2)
       Common Good
       — Friend should _____
                                    (3)
       _____
           because _____
                                    (4)
```

C Look at the Note-Taking Tips below. Did you use any of them when you took notes? Which were most helpful? How can you improve your notes the next time you listen to a lecture?

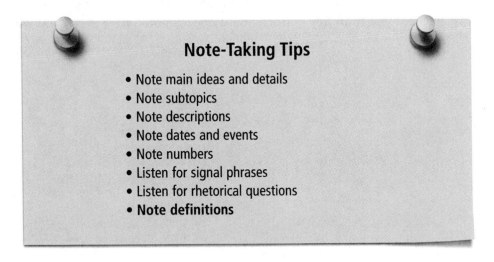

Note-Taking Tips

- Note main ideas and details
- Note subtopics
- Note descriptions
- Note dates and events
- Note numbers
- Listen for signal phrases
- Listen for rhetorical questions
- **Note definitions**

D Rewrite or revise your notes to make them clear. If you need to, listen to the lecture again.

Projects

1. Work in small groups. Discuss whether it is ethical to lie in each situation below. Explain the reasons for your opinion. Use the ethical principles from the lecture (or your own ethical principles) to justify your answers.

    a. Your friend asks you to come to a party. You don't want to go. You tell her you are going out of town.

    b. A friend gets an ugly haircut. You tell him it looks good.

    c. Your father is dying. You tell him he will get better.

    d. Your girlfriend/boyfriend says that she/he loves you. You don't feel the same way, but you say you love her/him, too.

    e. A man drops 50 dollars on the floor. You pick it up. When he looks for the money, you say you haven't seen it.

    f. The police want to arrest your neighbor because of his religious beliefs. You let him into your house, but you tell the police that he has left the city.

2. Find a current newspaper or magazine article about an ethical decision. For example, a leader must decide whether to go to war, or a business owner must decide whether to close a factory. Find out as much information as you can about the situation. Prepare a short report. Describe the ethical problem. Explain what you think the person should do (or should have done) and why.

A Good Night's Sleep

Topic Preview

Work in small groups. Discuss the questions below.

1. Look at the picture. Do you think this man sleeps well at night? Why or why not?

2. How well do you sleep? Check (✓) the box that best describes you. Compare your answers.

	Always	Sometimes	Never
a. I rarely feel tired.	❏	❏	❏
b. I stay up later than I should.	❏	❏	❏
c. I need an alarm clock to wake me up.	❏	❏	❏
d. I feel tired when I wake up.	❏	❏	❏
e. I go to bed as soon as I feel tired.	❏	❏	❏
f. I fall asleep during the day.	❏	❏	❏
g. I sleep more on weekends.	❏	❏	❏
h. I get enough sleep most nights.	❏	❏	❏

Vocabulary Preview

A The boldfaced words below are from a lecture about sleep. Read each sentence. Cross out the word or phrase that is *different* in meaning from the boldfaced word.

1. Feeling sleepy the next day is one ***consequence*** of going to bed late at night.
   a. cause
   b. effect
   c. result

2. You should get more sleep. Sleep ***deprivation*** can cause memory problems.
   a. lack of something
   b. quality of something
   c. not having something

3. One ***function*** of sleep is to help our brains relax. We sleep because our brains must rest for several hours each day.
   a. idea
   b. purpose
   c. job

4. I am in the ***habit*** of going to bed early. I am usually in bed by 9:00 P.M. every night.
   a. normal action
   b. usual activity
   c. rare action

5. I need a ***minimum*** of eight hours of sleep each night. If I get less sleep, I am very tired the next day.
   a. smallest amount
   b. highest amount
   c. least amount

6. Many sleep problems are ***related*** to other health problems, such as emotional stress.
   a. connected
   b. linked
   c. separated

7. Most runners ***require*** a good night's sleep before they run in a race. If they don't sleep well, they can't run fast.
   a. don't want
   b. need
   c. must have

8. Traffic safety experts now *recognize* that many auto accidents are caused by sleepy drivers.
   a. understand
   b. know
   c. decide

9. Many high school students stay up late and watch TV. They say they are sleepy during the day, and this *creates* problems at school.
   a. changes
   b. causes
   c. makes

10. A *survey* of 1,000 adults showed that 51% had trouble falling asleep at night.
    a. study
    b. answer
    c. questionnaire

B Complete each paragraph with correct boldfaced words.

Paragraph 1

> *consequence*　　　*habits*　　　*related*　　　*survey*

A _____ by the National Sleep Center (NSC) has given us
　　　　　　(1)
some interesting information about sleep. Every year, NSC asks people about
their sleep _____—how much they sleep, when they sleep, and
　　　　　　(2)
whether they have problems sleeping. One result of the study is that we now
know that some health problems are a _____ of not getting
　　　　　　　　　　　　　　　　　　　　(3)
enough sleep. We can also see how sleep problems are _____ to
　　　　　　　　　　　　　　　　　　　　　　　　　　　　(4)
other problems, such as stress.

Paragraph 2

> *function*　　　*minimum*　　　*require*

Our bodies _____ food and water to stay alive. We need a
　　　　　　　　(1)
_____ of one liter of water each day. With less water, the body will
　　(2)
not _____ well, and a person will become very sick.
　　　(3)

Paragraph 3

deprive　　　*recognize*　　　*creates*

Many people today eat too much fat. This _____ health
(1)
problems such as obesity. One source of the problem is fast food like
hamburgers and french fries. However, although we _____ that
(2)
eating a lot of fat is bad for us, we don't stop. We don't want to
_____ ourselves of our favorite foods.
(3)

C Listen to each sentence. Circle the word you hear.

1. recognize   deprive
2. creates   consequence
3. survey   habit
4. minimum   function
5. related   require
6. consequence   function
7. require   recognize
8. related   creates
9. survey   minimum
10. habit   deprivation

Taking Better Notes

Noting Causes and Effects

When giving lectures, speakers often use signal words or phrases to show causes or
reasons. They also often use words or phrases to introduce effects or results.

The boldfaced words below signal causes.

If I go to bed late, I am sleepy the next day.
I am sleepy *because* I got very little sleep last night.
Since I didn't go to bed until two in the morning, I fell asleep in class.

The boldfaced words below signal effects.

Sometimes I go to bed late. *As a result,* I am sleepy the next day.

Going to bed late *causes* problems in school for students.

Our modern lifestyle *creates* many of our sleep problems.

One way to show the relationship between a cause and its effect is to use an arrow (➔). The arrow points toward the effect.

Read the notes from a lecture about sleep problems. Notice how the student used arrows to show causes and effects. Also notice how the student used the symbols and abbreviations below.

% = percent	hrs. = hours
b.f. = before	/ = per; each
< = less than	

PUBLIC HEALTH: SLEEP

Bad sleep habits → teen sleep problems.

44% watch TV b.f. bed.

   → to bed late

35% drink soda with caffeine

   → don't sleep well

Most teens sleep < 8 hrs./night

   → 10% late-school

   → 60% tired

   → 15% fall asleep-class

Work with a partner. Use the above notes to answer the questions below.

1. What do many teenagers do before bed? What are the effects?

2. How much sleep do most teens get each night?

3. What happens to teens who do not get enough sleep?

When you listen to a lecture, listen for signal words or phrases for causes and effects. Try to use arrows to note causes and effects. Use symbols and abbreviations, if possible.

Listening to the Lecture

Before You Listen

You will hear a lecture about sleep deprivation. Write two things that might happen if you don't get enough sleep.

1. _____

2. _____

Listening for Main Ideas

A Close your book. Listen to the lecture and take notes.

B Use your notes to answer each question below. Check (✓) a, b, c, or d. Compare your answers in small groups.

1. What causes of sleep deprivation does the speaker mention?
   (*Check two answers.*)

   _____ **a.** working too much

   _____ **b.** sleeping in an uncomfortable bed

   _____ **c.** using modern technology

   _____ **d.** not being able to fall asleep at night

2. What consequences of sleep deprivation does the speaker mention?
   (*Check two answers.*)

   _____ **a.** problems in school

   _____ **b.** mistakes at work

   _____ **c.** car accidents

   _____ **d.** problems with health

Listening for Details

A Close your book. Listen to the lecture again. Add details to your notes and correct any mistakes.

B Use your notes to decide if the statements below are true or false. Write T (true) or F (false.) Correct the false statements.

_____ 1. Most people recognize that sleep deprivation is a serious health problem.

_____ 2. The survey results are from the National Sleep Center.

_____ 3. Sixty percent of Americans work more than fifty hours per week.

_____ 4. Forty-three percent of Americans stay up late reading or using the Internet.

_____ 5. Most people need eight hours of sleep per night.

_____ 6. Feeling sleepy when you wake up is a sign of sleep deprivation.

_____ 7. There are 50,000 sleep-related car accidents in the U.S. each year.

_____ 8. Seventeen percent of Americans report falling asleep while driving.

Using Your Notes

A Look at Before You Listen on page 74. Did the speaker discuss the things you wrote?

B Information is missing from the lecture notes below. Use your notes to complete them. Add details that explain the causes and effects of sleep deprivation.

SLEEP DEPRIVATION

    Causes

    Working too much

       —30% of Americans _____
                       (1)

        → _____
                 (2)

    Modern technology

       —Everything on _____
                   (3)

       → 45% _____
                (4)

Effects

Problems at work

　—50% _____
　　　　　　　　　　　　(5)

　—20% _____
　　　　　　　　　　　　(6)

Car accidents

　—100,000 _____
　　　　　　　　　　　　(7)

→ 71,000 _____ and 1,500 _____
　　　　　(8)　　　　　　　　　(9)

　—50% _____
　　　　　　　　　　　(10)

　—17% _____
　　　　　　　　　　　(11)

C Look at the Note-Taking Tips below. Did you use any of them when you took notes? Which were most helpful? How can you improve your notes the next time you listen to a lecture?

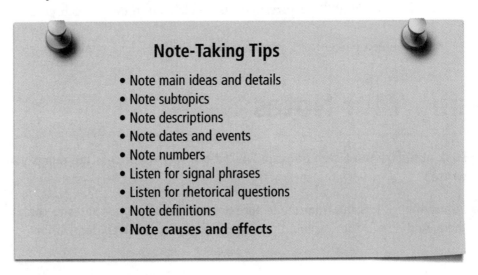

Note-Taking Tips

- Note main ideas and details
- Note subtopics
- Note descriptions
- Note dates and events
- Note numbers
- Listen for signal phrases
- Listen for rhetorical questions
- Note definitions
- **Note causes and effects**

D Rewrite or revise your notes to make them clear. If you need to, listen to the lecture again.

Projects

1. *Insomnia* is the problem of not being able to sleep. Work with a partner. Think of advice for people with insomnia. Make a poster listing things they should and shouldn't do. Use the lists below as a model. Then compare posters as a class.

Do	Don't
Drink herbal tea	Eat a lot before bed
Sleep in a quiet room	Sleep in an uncomfortable bed

2. Make a Sleep Diary. Use the diary below as a model. Write in your diary every morning for one week. Then discuss the questions that follow in a small group.

> **MONDAY, JUNE 4**
>
> Before I went to bed, I watched TV and ate ice cream. I went to bed at 11:30 p.m. I fell asleep around 11:40 p.m. I woke up 2 times—I was cold, then I heard a noise in the street. I woke up at 7 a.m. I had a total of 7 hrs. 20 mins. sleep. This morning I feel tired.

a. When did you get the most sleep? When did you get the least? Why?

b. When did you feel tired in the morning? When did you feel well rested? Why?

c. How did your activities before bed affect your sleep?

d. What can you do to sleep better at night?

Negotiating for Success

Topic Preview

Work in small groups. Discuss the questions below.

1. Look at the picture. What do you think these people are talking about? How do you think they feel?

2. A *negotiation* is a discussion between people who are trying to agree on something. Look at the types of negotiations below. Number them from 1 (easiest) to 6 (most difficult). Explain your answers.

   _____ A husband and wife are deciding where to go on vacation.

   _____ An employee is trying to get a pay raise from his boss.

   _____ A country is trying to stop a war with another country.

   _____ Two companies are trying to merge (join together).

   _____ A student is asking his teacher for more time to do a class project.

   _____ A teenager is asking to use his parents' car.

3. Think of a negotiation you have had with someone. What was the problem? How did you negotiate? What was the result?

Vocabulary Preview

A **The boldfaced words below are from a lecture about negotiation. Read each sentence. Match each word with its definition.**

_____ 1. Joe's wife is sick. Her problem *affects* Joe at work. He always feels worried and has trouble finishing projects on time.

_____ 2. I try to *avoid* long meetings at work. I try to keep my meetings short.

_____ 3. My boss *blames* me because I didn't finish the project. He said it was my fault.

_____ 4. A business does better when everyone can *communicate* clearly. Everyone must be able to talk and understand each other.

_____ 5. My co-worker and I have a *conflict* about how to finish a project. We don't agree about what to do.

---

a. a disagreement between people
b. to express thoughts and feelings
c. to think someone is responsible for something bad
d. to try not to do something
e. to cause a change in someone or something

_____ 6. I like to dream about having a different job. For example, sometimes I *imagine* that I am a singer in a rock and roll band.

_____ 7. My co-worker and I have a problem. We talked about the *issue* yesterday, but couldn't decide what to do.

_____ 8. My boss didn't *react* well when I told her the project was late. She got very angry and walked out of the room.

_____ 9. I don't know how to *solve* this problem. I don't know what we should do.

_____ 10. There are many *techniques* for negotiation. Today, we'll talk about one way to negotiate.

---

f. to behave a certain way because of someone's actions or words
g. to find an answer to something
h. a subject or problem that people think is important
i. to form pictures or ideas in your mind
j. a special way to do something

B Read each group of sentences. Circle the letter of the sentence closest in meaning to the first sentence.

1. My company's problems affect me.
   a. I feel worried and upset.
   b. I don't feel anything.

2. I blame my boss for my problems at work.
   a. I think my boss caused the problems.
   b. I don't think my boss caused the problems.

3. I communicate well with my co-workers.
   a. We don't understand each other.
   b. We can talk together easily.

4. I hate conflict.
   a. I hate to disagree with people.
   b. I like to argue about my opinion.

5. Sometimes I imagine being a millionaire.
   a. I am a millionaire.
   b. I think about being a millionaire.

6. We discussed the issue during the meeting.
   a. We discussed the subject.
   b. We discussed the news.

7. My co-worker's phone rang, but he didn't react.
   a. He didn't do anything.
   b. He answered the phone.

8. We finally solved the problem.
   a. We found an answer.
   b. We didn't know what to do.

9. Exercise is a good technique for lowering stress.
   a. It's a good reason for lowering stress.
   b. It's a good way to lower stress.

10. I avoid talking to her.
    a. I like to talk to her.
    b. I try not to talk to her.

C Listen to each sentence and repeat it. Try to pronounce the boldfaced word correctly.

1. Everyone should *communicate* clearly.

2. I don't know how to *solve* this problem.

3. I try to *avoid* long meetings.

4. My boss *blames* me for the problem.

5. My boss didn't *react* well to my report.

6. My co-worker and I have a *conflict*.

7. Sometimes I *imagine* that I'm a singer.

8. The problem *affects* Joe at work.

9. There are many *techniques* for negotiation.

10. We talked about the *issue*.

Taking Better Notes

Noting Examples

When giving lectures, speakers often give examples to illustrate the most important ideas or to make them more real. The signal phrases below are used to introduce examples.

For instance, . . .
Now let's imagine that . . .
Let's say that . . .
For example, . . .
An example is . . .

When noting examples, it may be helpful to list them below the ideas they illustrate. You can also list them next to the ideas.

Read the notes from a lecture about negotiation. Notice how the student used the symbol below.

ex. = example

NEGOTIATION

Places We Negotiate:

    Business

        ex.—agreement to sell

        ex.— _____
                       (1)

    School

        ex.—choosing a class project

        ex.— _____
                       (2)

    Family

        ex.— _____
                       (3)

        ex.— _____
                       (4)

The above notes are missing information. Complete them with the examples below.

choosing a TV game show   handing in homework late
joining two companies   where to go on vacation

When you listen to a lecture, try to note examples. Use symbols and abbreviations, if possible.

Listening to the Lecture

Before You Listen

You will hear a lecture about business negotiation. Write two pieces of advice you think the speaker might give.

1. _____

2. _____

Listening for Main Ideas

A Close your book. Listen to the lecture and take notes.

B Use your notes to complete the statements below. Circle a, b, or c. Compare your answers in small groups.

1. In a negotiation, it is important to _____.
    a. tell the other person about the conflict
    b. avoid blaming the other person for the problem
    c. solve the problem as quickly as possible

2. A good negotiation technique is using _____ statements.
    a. "I"
    b. "you"
    c. "we"

3. Problems in negotiation are usually caused by _____.
    a. the people in the negotiation
    b. the issues in the negotiation
    c. how people feel about the negotiation

Listening for Details

A Close your book. Listen to the lecture again. Add details to your notes and correct any mistakes.

B Use your notes to complete the statements below. Circle a or b.

1. The example in the lecture _____.
    a. is imagined by the speaker
    b. really happened to the speaker

2. In the example, Joe _____ his work on time.
    a. is finishing
    b. isn't finishing

3. Blaming people often _____ a negotiation.
    a. helps
    b. stops

4. The speaker says we should use "I" statements to avoid _____ the other person.
    a. talking to
    b. blaming

5. Instead of saying "You aren't doing your work," we should say _____.
   a. "I think the work isn't done."
   b. "I'm worried because the work isn't done."

6. Instead of saying "The project will be late because of you," we should say _____.
   a. "I'm afraid that the project will be late."
   b. "I'm going to be late finishing the project."

Using Your Notes

A Look at Before You Listen on page 82. Did the speaker give the advice you wrote?

B The lecture notes below are missing examples. Use your notes to complete them.

BUSINESS: NEGOTIATION TECHNIQUES

CONFLICT AT WORK

   Ex. w/co-worker

     Blame

     ex. "_____"
                    (1)

        → co-worker angry, upset

        → won't _____
                      (2)

     Avoid blame—use _____ statements
                 (3)

     ex. "_____"
                    (4)

        → co-worker not angry

   Another ex.

     Blame

     ex. "The project is going to be late

       because _____"
                 (5)

     Avoid blame

     ex. "I'm afraid that _____"
                    (6)

C Look at the Note-Taking Tips below. Did you use any of them when you took notes? Which were most helpful? How can you improve your notes the next time you listen to a lecture?

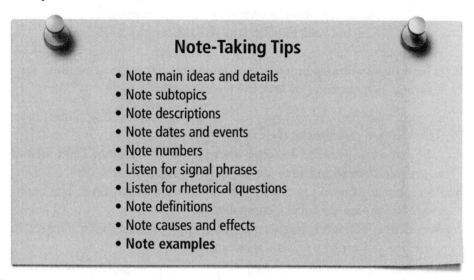

Note-Taking Tips

- Note main ideas and details
- Note subtopics
- Note descriptions
- Note dates and events
- Note numbers
- Listen for signal phrases
- Listen for rhetorical questions
- Note definitions
- Note causes and effects
- **Note examples**

D Rewrite or revise your notes to make them clear. If you need to, listen to the lecture again.

Projects

1. Different cultures use different styles of negotiation. Read the tips for negotiating with American business people.

> **Tips for Negotiating with Americans**
>
> 1. Try to negotiate so both sides will "win" and be happy with the solution.
> 2. Imagine how the people on the other side see the conflict.
> 3. To show you are listening, keep eye contact when someone is talking to you.
> 4. Paraphrase (repeat) statements by the other side to show you understand.
> 5. Tell the truth as much as you can.
> 6. Use "I" statements to explain how the problem affects you.
> 7. If there are a lot of emotions during the negotiation, talk about your feelings and ask people on the other side about their feelings.
> 8. Be polite. Don't get angry and yell.

Then choose another culture you want to know more about. Conduct library or Internet research about how people negotiate in that culture. Then discuss the questions below in a small group.

a. Which American negotiation techniques are appropriate in the other culture? Which are not? Explain why. Give examples to illustrate your opinion.

b. Which negotiation techniques from the other culture do you think are helpful? Give examples of how the techniques are used.

2. Work with a partner. Create a role play based on one of the situations below. Perform the role play for the class.

a. A husband and wife are deciding where to go on vacation. The husband wants to go skiing and the wife wants to go to the beach.

b. An employee is trying to get a pay raise from his or her boss. The boss needs to save money for the company.

c. A student is asking his teacher for more time to do a project. The teacher wants the project to be finished on time.

d. A teenager is asking to use his or her parents' car to go to a friend's house. The parents need to use the car to go shopping.

Statistics

Risking It

Topic Preview

Work in small groups. Discuss the questions below.

1. Look at the pictures. What do you think these people are doing? Which activities are risky (dangerous)? Why are they risky?

2. How risky are the following activities? Label each activity H (high risk), M (medium risk), or L (low risk).

   _____ Going near a nuclear power plant

   _____ Driving a car

   _____ Smoking cigarettes

   _____ Going swimming

   _____ Going mountain climbing

   _____ Flying in an airplane

3. Are you a *risk-taker* (someone who enjoys doing dangerous things) or do you prefer to *play it safe* (not take risks)? Describe something risky you have done. How did you feel about it?

Vocabulary Preview

A The boldfaced words below are from a lecture about taking risks. Read each paragraph. Match each boldfaced word with its definition.

Paragraph 1

Driving a car is an (1) **everyday** activity, so most people don't think much about the risk. However, sometimes terrible accidents (2) **occur**, events that can (3) **injure** or even kill people. Driving a car is (4) **perceived** as safe—most of us don't worry when we get into a car. However, the (5) **actual** risks of driving a car are high.

_____ **a.** real and clear

_____ **b.** understood in a particular way

_____ **c.** to happen

_____ **d.** to harm or wound

_____ **e.** usual

Paragraph 2

Many people live in (1) **circumstances** that create risk. However, different factors affect whether people worry about the risk. One factor is whether they see it as high risk (2) **versus** low risk. Most people worry about risk only when there is a (3) **significant** danger—when the risks become very high. Some risks are (4) **natural**, such as bad weather or earthquakes. We cannot (5) **control** these risks because we don't have the power to change the weather or stop earthquakes.

_____ **a.** the ability to make something do what you want

_____ **b.** noticeable or important

_____ **c.** in contrast to

_____ **d.** not made by people or machines

_____ **e.** the conditions that affect a situation

B Complete the sentences with the correct words below.

circumstances	perceives	injuries	versus	significant
everyday	actual	natural	occur	control

1. Everyone _____ risk differently. We all have different opinions about risky activities.

2. Many _____ at work are caused when people do not follow safety rules.

3. Some _____ make driving a car more dangerous, such as driving on wet or snowy roads.

4. We don't think much about _____ risks such as crossing the street or falling down in the bathtub.

5. We compared high risk _____ low risk activities.

6. Smoking is a serious health problem. Smokers have a _____ risk of getting cancer.

7. Some people want to eat only _____ food, grown without any chemicals, because they think it is healthier.

8. Mountain climbing seems dangerous, but the _____ risk of injury is low.

9. Driving a truck is a risky job because many accidents _____ on the road.

10. Car accidents happen when drivers can't _____ their car.

C You will hear each word below in a sentence. Listen to the sentences. Write the number of the sentence that contains each word.

_____ everyday   _____ injure

_____ control   _____ circumstances

_____ natural   _____ actual

_____ occur   _____ significant

_____ versus   _____ perceive

Taking Better Notes

Noting Comparisons and Contrasts

Lectures often include comparisons and contrasts. It is important to note how items are similar or different.

The boldfaced phrases below signal that two things are being compared or contrasted.

Let's look at riding a bicycle $\left\{\begin{array}{c} \textit{as opposed to} \\ \textit{versus} \end{array}\right\}$ driving a car.

The boldfaced phrases below show how the things are similar or different.

Riding a bicycle is $\left\{\begin{array}{c} \textit{more dangerous than} \\ \textit{riskier than} \\ \textit{less safe than} \\ \textit{not as safe as} \\ \textit{as fun as} \end{array}\right\}$ driving a car.

The lecture notes below compare risk of death for different groups of people. Notice how the student used arrows to show an increase or decrease in risk. Also, notice how the student used the abbreviations and symbols below.

vs. = versus   ↑ increase   ↓ decrease

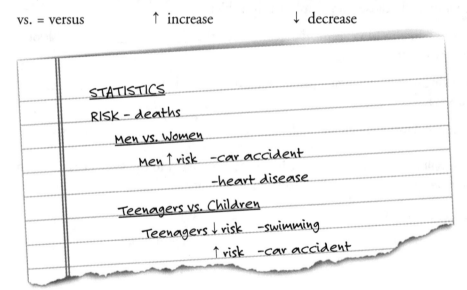

STATISTICS
RISK – deaths
Men vs. Women
 Men ↑ risk –car accident
              –heart disease
Teenagers vs. Children
 Teenagers ↓ risk –swimming
           ↑ risk –car accident

Circle the word that best completes the statements about the above notes.

1. Men have a <u>higher / lower</u> risk of dying in a car accident than women.

2. Compared to men, women have a <u>higher / lower</u> risk of dying from heart disease.

3. Swimming is <u>more / less</u> dangerous for children than for teenagers.

4. For teenagers, riding in a car is probably <u>riskier than / not as risky as</u> swimming.

When you listen to a lecture, try to note comparisons and contrasts.

Listening to the Lecture

Before You Listen

You will hear a lecture about risk. Write two risky activities you think the speaker might discuss.

1. _____

2. _____

Listening for Main Ideas

A Close your book. Listen to the lecture and take notes.

B Use your notes. Put the topics in the order discussed in the lecture. Number the topics from 1 to 4. Compare your answers in small groups.

_____ Activities we control versus activities we don't control

_____ Unusual events versus everyday activities

_____ Perceived risk versus actual risk

_____ Natural risks versus unnatural risks

Listening for Details

A Close your book. Listen to the lecture again. Add details to your notes and correct any mistakes.

B Use your notes to complete the statements below. Circle a or b.

1. Our perception of risk is _____ the actual risk of an activity.
   a. often very different from
   b. usually the same as

2. The actual risk of driving is _____ than the actual risk of flying.
   a. lower
   b. higher

3. We perceive risk differently _____.
   a. in different circumstances
   b. for different people

4. We feel that activities we control are _____ risky than activities we don't control.
   a. less
   b. more

5. We feel that natural risks are _____ risky than unnatural risks.
   a. less
   b. more

6. We feel that unusual events are _____ risky than everyday activities.
   a. less
   b. more

Using Your Notes

A Look at Before You Listen on page 91. Did the speaker discuss the activities you wrote?

B Work with a partner. The lecture notes below are missing information. Use your notes to complete them.

STATISTICS: Risk

Perceived vs. Actual Risk

   ex. Driving vs. flying

      Perceived Risk: driving ↓

              flying ↑

    _____ : driving ↑
         (1)

              flying ↓

Circumstances Change Perceived Risk

   1. Control vs. _____
                 (2)

      ex. Driving vs. flying

            _____ : feel ↓ risk
            (3)

   2. _____ vs. unnatural
        (4)

      ex. Out in sun vs. near nuclear power plant

            _____ : feel ↓ risk
            (5)

   3. _____
        (6)

      ex. Accidents at home vs. airplane accidents

            _____ : feel ↓ risk
            (7)

C Look at the Note-Taking Tips below. Did you use any of them when you took notes? Which were most helpful? How can you improve your notes the next time you listen to a lecture?

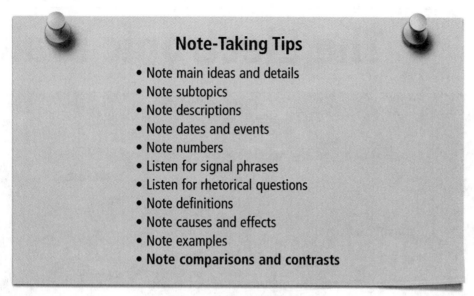

Note-Taking Tips

- Note main ideas and details
- Note subtopics
- Note descriptions
- Note dates and events
- Note numbers
- Listen for signal phrases
- Listen for rhetorical questions
- Note definitions
- Note causes and effects
- Note examples
- **Note comparisons and contrasts**

D Rewrite or revise your notes to make them clear. If you need to, listen to the lecture again.

Projects

1. Work in small groups. Make a list of ten activities with different levels of risk. Use examples from the lecture and your own ideas. Number the activities from 1 (least risky) to 10 (most risky). Discuss why some activities have a higher perceived risk or a higher actual risk.

2. Interview three people outside of class. Circle Male or Female. Ask them to rate the activities in the chart below as high risk (H), medium risk (M) or low risk (L). Write the answers in the chart.

	Male/Female	Male/Female	Male/Female
Driving a car			
Flying			
Being in the sun			
Being near nuclear power			

Then compare your answers in small groups. Did people perceive the risks in the same way? Explain.

The Electronic Brain

Topic Preview

Work in small groups. Discuss the questions below.

1. Look at the picture. When do you think it was taken?

2. How big do you think this computer was?

3. What do you think this computer could do?

4. This computer was called *ENIAC*. Some people also called it the *Electronic Brain*. Why do you think they used this name?

Vocabulary Preview

A The boldfaced words below are from a lecture about computers. Read each paragraph. Match each boldfaced word with the correct definition.

Paragraph 1

A computer is a (1) *complex* machine. Each part is very complicated. Over the years, many (2) *engineers* have worked to develop better computers. They (3) *designed* how each part worked. Sometimes their plans could not be built because of the limits of (4) *technology*. Scientists did not yet have the information or equipment to build it. However, technology has changed a lot over the past few years. Today we can build computers that are much more complicated than the ones built in (5) *previous* years.

_____ **a.** happening before the present time

_____ **b.** having many closely connected parts or processes

_____ **c.** people who plan the way things are built

_____ **d.** knowledge and equipment used in science and making machines

_____ **e.** made a drawing as a plan for something

Paragraph 2

I did some (1) *calculations* on how much money I spent last year. There were many (2) *elements* to this problem, such as the amount I spent on food, housing, and clothing. I added up the amount I spent on each thing, and found the total. I don't have an electric calculator, so I had to do the math (3) *by hand*, with pencil and paper. However, I'm afraid I've made an (4) *error*, and the result is wrong. My friend knows how to (5) *program* a computer to solve this type of problem. We are going to use the computer to get the right answer.

_____ **a.** parts of a whole

_____ **b.** a mistake

_____ **c.** by a person, not a machine

_____ **d.** using numbers to find an answer

_____ **e.** to give a computer instructions

B Read each sentence. Choose the word from the box that is closest in meaning to the boldfaced word or phrase. Write the word on the line.

an error	by hand	calculation	complex	design
elements	engineer	previous	program	technology

1. What was the *amount* you got after adding everything up? _____

2. I'll *give instructions to* the computer to solve the problem. _____

3. I did all the problems *without using a machine*. _____

4. I'm sorry. There is *a mistake* on this test. _____

5. In my *earlier* job, I worked for a computer company. _____

6. In the past 100 years, *scientific knowledge* has improved a lot. _____

7. They are going to *make plans to build* better telephones. _____

8. The *person who made the plan* will fix the computer. _____

9. There are many electronic *parts* in a computer. _____

10. This is a *complicated* machine to fix. _____

C Listen to each sentence. Circle the word you hear.

1. complex   previous

2. error   engineer

3. by hand   previous

4. complex   by hand

5. engineer   technology

6. elements   error

7. design   program

8. design   program

9. technology   calculations

10. calculations   elements

Taking Better Notes

Choosing the Best Note-Taking Techniques

To take better notes, it is important to understand how you learn. A note-taking or review technique that is very helpful for one person might not be helpful for another.

Evaluate each note-taking technique below. Check (✓) Very Helpful, Somewhat Helpful, or Not Helpful.

	Very Helpful	Somewhat Helpful	Not Helpful
a. Make an outline of the lecture	❏	❏	❏
b. Take detailed notes	❏	❏	❏
c. Make charts and drawings	❏	❏	❏
d. Note only main ideas and add examples later	❏	❏	❏
e. Listen without taking notes	❏	❏	❏

Evaluate each review technique below. Check (✓) Very Helpful, Somewhat Helpful, or Not Helpful.

	Very Helpful	Somewhat Helpful	Not Helpful
a. Ask the teacher questions	❏	❏	❏
b. Discuss the lecture with other students	❏	❏	❏
c. Rewrite my notes	❏	❏	❏
d. Revise my notes	❏	❏	❏
e. Summarize the main ideas in short paragraphs	❏	❏	❏
f. Make note cards	❏	❏	❏
g. Make charts or drawings	❏	❏	❏
h. Compare notes with other students	❏	❏	❏

Compare your answers in small groups. What other note-taking or review techniques are helpful for you?

Before you listen to a lecture, think about what note-taking and review techniques work best for you.

Listening to the Lecture

Before You Listen

You will hear a lecture about ENIAC, the first electronic computer. Check (✓) the topics you think the speaker might discuss.

_____ Why the computer was built

_____ What computers were built later

_____ What the computer could do

_____ How much the computer cost

Listening for Main Ideas

A Close your book. Listen to the lecture and take notes.

B Use your notes. Complete each topic discussed in the lecture. Circle the letter that best completes each topic. Compare your answers in small groups.

1. The reasons why _____
   a. ENIAC was built
   b. it was hard to build ENIAC

2. The men who _____
   a. designed and built ENIAC
   b. paid for ENIAC

3. A description of _____
   a. what ENIAC looked like
   b. how much ENIAC cost

4. The type of _____
   a. computers built after ENIAC
   b. calculations ENIAC could do

Listening for Details

A Close your book. Listen to the lecture again. Add details to your notes and correct any mistakes.

B Use your notes to decide if the statements below are true or false. Write T (true) or F (false). Correct the false statements.

_____ 1. The ENIAC project was started at the beginning of World War II.

_____ 2. The American company IBM wanted a computer to do faster calculations.

_____ 3. John Mauchly and J. Presper Eckert were engineers for the ENIAC project.

_____ 4. John Mauchly was a 21-year-old physicist who was interested in the weather.

_____ 5. J. Presper Eckert was a 24-year-old Ph.D. student who loved building complex machines.

_____ 6. ENIAC filled 1,800 square feet, the size of a three-bedroom apartment.

_____ 7. ENIAC could do 5,000 calculations per minute.

_____ 8. ENIAC was finished in 1945.

_____ 9. Mauchly and Eckert made a lot of money from their work with computers.

_____ 10. ENIAC was used until 1963.

Using Your Notes

A Look at Before You Listen on page 98. Did the speaker discuss the topics you checked?

B Work in small groups. Use your notes to answer the questions below.

1. When and where was ENIAC built?

2. Why was it built?

3. Who was John Mauchly?

4. Who was J. Presper Eckert?

5. What did ENIAC look like?

6. What could it do?

7. What happened to the engineers after they finished the ENIAC project?

8. How long was ENIAC used?

C Look at the Note-Taking Tips below. Did you use any of them when you took notes? Which were most helpful? How can you improve your notes the next time you listen to a lecture?

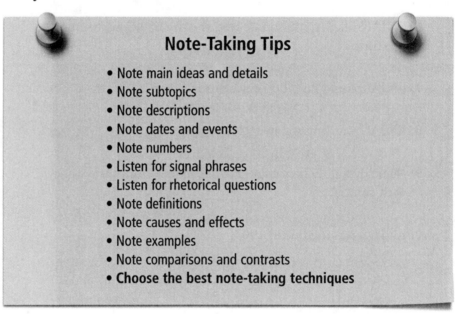

Note-Taking Tips

- Note main ideas and details
- Note subtopics
- Note descriptions
- Note dates and events
- Note numbers
- Listen for signal phrases
- Listen for rhetorical questions
- Note definitions
- Note causes and effects
- Note examples
- Note comparisons and contrasts
- **Choose the best note-taking techniques**

D Look at the note-taking and review techniques on page 97. What note-taking techniques were most helpful for this lecture? What review techniques do you think will be most helpful? Use these techniques to review the lecture.

Projects

1. What positive changes have computers made in our lives? What negative changes have they made? Work in small groups. Complete the chart below.

	Positive Changes	Negative Changes
School	Information from Internet	Don't learn to spell— computer spell-checker corrects the errors
Home		
Work		
Entertainment		

2. Use the Internet or library to research another important technological invention (for example, the light bulb, telephone, or CD player). Answer the following questions.
   a. When was it invented?
   b. Where was it invented?
   c. Who invented it?
   d. Why was it invented?
   e. How was it invented?

Write a short report about the invention. Share it with the class.

Appendix A: Academic Word List

Numbers indicate the sublist of the Academic Word List (for example, *abandon* and its family members are in Sublist 8). Sublist 1 contains the most frequent words in the list, and Sublist 10 contains the least frequent.

abandon	8	approach	1	chart	8
abstract	6	appropriate	2	chemical	7
academy	5	approximate	4	circumstance	3
access	4	arbitrary	8	cite	6
accommodate	9	area	1	civil	4
accompany	8	aspect	2	clarify	8
accumulate	8	assemble	10	classic	7
accurate	6	assess	1	clause	5
achieve	2	assign	6	code	4
acknowledge	6	assist	2	coherent	9
acquire	2	assume	1	coincide	9
adapt	7	assure	9	collapse	10
adequate	4	attach	6	colleague	10
adjacent	10	attain	9	commence	9
adjust	5	attitude	4	comment	3
administrate	2	attribute	4	commission	2
adult	7	author	6	commit	4
advocate	7	authority	1	commodity	8
affect	2	automate	8	communicate	4
aggregate	6	available	1	community	2
aid	7	aware	5	compatible	9
albeit	10	behalf	9	compensate	3
allocate	6	benefit	1	compile	10
alter	5	bias	8	complement	8
alternative	3	bond	6	complex	2
ambiguous	8	brief	6	component	3
amend	5	bulk	9	compound	5
analogy	9	capable	6	comprehensive	7
analyze	1	capacity	5	comprise	7
annual	4	category	2	compute	2
anticipate	9	cease	9	conceive	10
apparent	4	challenge	5	concentrate	4
append	8	channel	7	concept	1
appreciate	8	chapter	2	conclude	2

concurrent	9	crucial	8	drama	8
conduct	2	culture	2	duration	9
confer	4	currency	8	dynamic	7
confine	9	cycle	4	economy	1
confirm	7	data	1	edit	6
conflict	5	debate	4	element	2
conform	8	decade	7	eliminate	7
consent	3	decline	5	emerge	4
consequent	2	deduce	3	emphasis	3
considerable	3	define	1	empirical	7
consist	1	definite	7	enable	5
constant	3	demonstrate	3	encounter	10
constitute	1	denote	8	energy	5
constrain	3	deny	7	enforce	5
construct	2	depress	10	enhance	6
consult	5	derive	1	enormous	10
consume	2	design	2	ensure	3
contact	5	despite	4	entity	5
contemporary	8	detect	8	environment	1
context	1	deviate	8	equate	2
contract	1	device	9	equip	7
contradict	8	devote	9	equivalent	5
contrary	7	differentiate	7	erode	9
contrast	4	dimension	4	error	4
contribute	3	diminish	9	establish	1
controversy	9	discrete	5	estate	6
convene	3	discriminate	6	estimate	1
converse	9	displace	8	ethic	9
convert	7	display	6	ethnic	4
convince	10	dispose	7	evaluate	2
cooperate	6	distinct	2	eventual	8
coordinate	3	distort	9	evident	1
core	3	distribute	1	evolve	5
corporate	3	diverse	6	exceed	6
correspond	3	document	3	exclude	3
couple	7	domain	6	exhibit	8
create	1	domestic	4	expand	5
credit	2	dominate	3	expert	6
criteria	3	draft	5	explicit	6

exploit	8	hypothesis	4	integral	9
export	1	identical	7	integrate	4
expose	5	identify	1	integrity	10
external	5	ideology	7	intelligence	6
extract	7	ignorance	6	intense	8
facilitate	5	illustrate	3	interact	3
factor	1	image	5	intermediate	9
feature	2	immigrate	3	internal	4
federal	6	impact	2	interpret	1
fee	6	implement	4	interval	6
file	7	implicate	4	intervene	7
final	2	implicit	8	intrinsic	10
finance	1	imply	3	invest	2
finite	7	impose	4	investigate	4
flexible	6	incentive	6	invoke	10
fluctuate	8	incidence	6	involve	1
focus	2	incline	10	isolate	7
format	9	income	1	issue	1
formula	1	incorporate	6	item	2
forthcoming	10	index	6	job	4
foundation	7	indicate	1	journal	2
found	9	individual	1	justify	3
framework	3	induce	8	label	4
function	1	inevitable	8	labor	1
fund	3	infer	7	layer	3
fundamental	5	infrastructure	8	lecture	6
furthermore	6	inherent	9	legal	1
gender	6	inhibit	6	legislate	1
generate	5	initial	3	levy	10
generation	5	initiate	6	liberal	5
globe	7	injure	2	license	5
goal	4	innovate	7	likewise	10
grade	7	input	6	link	3
grant	4	insert	7	locate	3
guarantee	7	insight	9	logic	5
guideline	8	inspect	8	maintain	2
hence	4	instance	3	major	1
hierarchy	7	institute	2	manipulate	8
highlight	8	instruct	6	manual	9

margin	5	ongoing	10	primary	2
mature	9	option	4	prime	5
maximize	3	orient	5	principal	4
mechanism	4	outcome	3	principle	1
media	7	output	4	prior	4
mediate	9	overall	4	priority	7
medical	5	overlap	9	proceed	1
medium	9	overseas	6	process	1
mental	5	panel	10	professional	4
method	1	paradigm	7	prohibit	7
migrate	6	paragraph	8	project	4
military	9	parallel	4	promote	4
minimal	9	parameter	4	proportion	3
minimize	8	participate	2	prospect	8
minimum	6	partner	3	protocol	9
ministry	6	passive	9	psychology	5
minor	3	perceive	2	publication	7
mode	7	percent	1	publish	3
modify	5	period	1	purchase	2
monitor	5	persist	10	pursue	5
motive	6	perspective	5	qualitative	9
mutual	9	phase	4	quote	7
negate	3	phenomenon	7	radical	8
network	5	philosophy	3	random	8
neutral	6	physical	3	range	2
nevertheless	6	plus	8	ratio	5
nonetheless	10	policy	1	rational	6
norm	9	portion	9	react	3
normal	2	pose	10	recover	6
notion	5	positive	2	refine	9
notwithstanding	10	potential	2	regime	4
nuclear	8	practitioner	8	region	2
objective	5	precede	6	register	3
obtain	2	precise	5	regulate	2
obvious	4	predict	4	reinforce	8
occupy	4	predominant	8	reject	5
occur	1	preliminary	9	relax	9
odd	10	presume	6	release	7
offset	8	previous	2	relevant	2

reluctance	10	sole	7	text	2
rely	3	somewhat	7	theme	8
remove	3	source	1	theory	1
require	1	specific	1	thereby	8
research	1	specify	3	thesis	7
reside	2	sphere	9	topic	7
resolve	4	stable	5	trace	6
resource	2	statistic	4	tradition	2
respond	1	status	4	transfer	2
restore	8	straightforward	10	transform	6
restrain	9	strategy	2	transit	5
restrict	2	stress	4	transmit	7
retain	4	structure	1	transport	6
reveal	6	style	5	trend	5
revenue	5	submit	7	trigger	9
reverse	7	subordinate	9	ultimate	7
revise	8	subsequent	4	undergo	10
revolution	9	subsidy	6	underlie	6
rigid	9	substitute	5	undertake	4
role	1	successor	7	uniform	8
route	9	sufficient	3	unify	9
scenario	9	sum	4	unique	7
schedule	8	summary	4	utilize	6
scheme	3	supplement	9	valid	3
scope	6	survey	2	vary	1
section	1	survive	7	vehicle	8
sector	1	suspend	9	version	5
secure	2	sustain	5	via	8
seek	2	symbol	5	violate	9
select	2	tape	6	virtual	8
sequence	3	target	5	visible	7
series	4	task	3	vision	9
sex	3	team	9	visual	8
shift	3	technical	3	volume	3
significant	1	technique	3	voluntary	7
similar	1	technology	3	welfare	5
simulate	7	temporary	9	whereas	5
site	2	tense	8	whereby	10
so-called	10	terminate	8	widespread	8

Appendix B: Affix Charts

Learning the meanings of affixes can help you identify unfamiliar words you read or hear. A *prefix* is a letter or group of letters added to the beginning of a word. It usually changes the meaning. A *suffix* is a letter or group of letters at the end of a word. It usually changes the part of speech.

The charts below contain common prefixes and suffixes. Refer to the chart as you use this book.

Prefixes

Meaning	Prefixes	Examples
not, without	a-, ab-, il-, im-, in-, ir-, un-	atypical, abnormal, illegal, impossible, inconvenient, irregular, unfair
opposed to, against	anti-	antisocial, antiseptic
with, together	co-, col-, com-, con-, cor-	coexist, collect, commune, connect, correct
give something the opposite quality	de-	decriminalize
not, remove	dis-	disapprove, disarm
no longer, former	ex-	ex-wife, ex-president
out, from	ex-	export, exit
outside, beyond	extra-	extracurricular, extraordinary
in, into	im-, in-	import, incoming
between, among	inter-	international
later than, after	post-	postgraduate
in favor of	pro-	pro-education
half, partly	semi-	semicircle, semi-literate
under, below, less important	sub-	subway, submarine, subordinate
larger, greater, stronger	super-	supermarket, supervisor

Suffixes

Meaning	Suffixes	Examples
having the quality of, capable of (adj)	-able, -ible	comfortable, responsible
relating to (adj)	-al, -ial	professional, ceremonial
the act, state, or quality of (n)	-ance, -ence, -ancy, -ency	performance, intelligence, conservancy, competency
the act, state, or result of (n)	-ation, -tion, -ion	examination, selection, facilitation
someone who does a particular thing (n)	-ar, -er, -or, -ist	beggar, photographer, editor, psychologist
full of (adj)	-ful	beautiful, harmful, fearful
give something a particular quality (v)	-ify, -ize	clarify, modernize
the quality of (n)	-ility	affordability, responsibility, humility
a political or religious belief system	-ism	atheism, capitalism
relating to (or someone who has) a political or religious belief (adj, n)	-ist	Buddhist, socialist
having a particular quality (adj)	-ive, -ous, -ious	creative, dangerous, mysterious
a particular quality (n)	-ity	popularity, creativity
without (adj)	-less	careless, worthless
in a particular way (adj)	-ly	briefly, fluently
conditions that result from something (n)	-ment	government, development
quality of (n)	-ness	happiness, seriousness